What's the Deal With Estate Administration?

By
PEGGY R. HOYT, J.D., M.B.A.

People Tested
M E D I A

Contents

CHAPTER ONE

First Things First— What Do I Do When a Loved One Dies?

Death never comes at the right time, despite what mortals believe. Death always comes like a thief.

~ Christopher Pike

When you lose someone you love, whether suddenly or after a long illness, you are never fully prepared. It's difficult to know what to do first. You might feel like you've been dropped off in a foreign country where you don't speak the language. You may be lost, sad and often confused and overwhelmed.

First, it is important to allow yourself to grieve. Emotions of grief include sadness, relief, anger, frustration and denial. It is a process that may be very difficult, primarily because you don't want to feel the unbearable sadness and emptiness that losing a loved one brings. Give yourself the time to really feel all the emotions that accompany a great loss.

Although the process of grieving may take a long time, there can be a lot to do when someone dies. You have to contact family and friends. You have to complete final funeral arrangements. You have to arrange for the care of surviving family members and pets. You have to secure real and personal property. And, these are just a few of the seemingly thousands of things that must be done.

You might not want to, or feel like doing any of these things. You may just want to pull the covers over your head. Yet, the things to do when someone dies remain. If you have close friends or family, accept their offers of help with gratitude. They can help accomplish many tasks that don't require your personal attention.

When it's time to get down to the business of settling someone's estate, there are essentially three steps.

Step one is to identify, gather and value the assets of the estate. This includes determining how assets were owned and whether there were any named beneficiaries. This step can be easy or hard depending on how organized the decedent was during their life time.

Step two is to identify and pay the creditors of the estate, including any taxes that may be due. This part of the administration process may actually take the longest.

Step three is to distribute all remaining assets to the beneficiaries of the estate. Determining the identity of the beneficiaries may be easy or hard depending on whether there was a will or trust with written instructions or whether the laws of the state of residence will apply.

Every estate administration requires the same three steps. Some will be easier than others. Some families will work together to achieve a common goal. Some estates will result in family disharmony. Some may even result in litigation.

First Things First

In order to fully understand the nature of a person's estate, you'll need to gather all of your loved one's important papers. Look for the following:

1. **Financial Documents**

   - Bank Statements
   - Investment Statements
   - Retirement Account Statements
   - Pension Statements
   - Annuity Account Statements
   - Life Insurance Policies
   - Beneficiary Designation Forms
   - Deeds for Real Estate
   - Titles to all Vehicles including Automobiles, RVs and Boats
   - Stock and Bond Certificates
   - Personal Income Tax Returns (last two years)
   - Prenuptial or Postnuptial Agreements
   - Loan Papers

2. **Business Documents**

   - Corporate, LLC or Partnership Documents, including buy-sell agreements
   - Contracts
   - Leases
   - Business Owned Life Insurance
   - Business Income Tax Returns (last two years)

3. Bills and Potential Creditors

- Utility Bills (cable, internet, phone, gas, water, electric)
- Cell Phone Bill
- Credit Card Bills
- Mortgages and Personal Loan Papers
- Real Estate Tax Bills
- Storage Unit Bills
- Medical Bills
- Nursing home bills
- Funeral Bills

Finding bills is a good way to identify creditors that may need to be paid or credit cards that need to be cancelled. Often, however, these documents can be difficult to locate, as many bills now come via electronic transmission. If you have access, you may also want to check your loved one's emails.

4. Estate Planning Documents

- Last Will and Testament and any Codicils
- Revocable Living Trust and any Amendments
- Irrevocable Trusts
- Gift Tax Returns (all)
- Any other documents related to your loved one's estate plan

You will also need to obtain multiple original death certificates (both short and long forms that reflect or omit the cause of death—depending on your state). A good rule of thumb is to start with five short forms and five long forms. Some states prohibit recording a death certificate that reflects the cause of death for privacy reasons. However, most insurance companies want death certificates that reflect the cause of death in case there are exclusionary clauses in a policy. Most institutions only need to make a copy of a death certificate and don't need to keep the original. For recording in the public property records or filing with the probate court, originals will be required.

Certain notifications must also be made with information that includes the decedent's name, social security number, date of death, whether the death was due to accident or illness, and your name and address. Necessary notifications may include the following:

- Employer provided employee benefits, such as life insurance, pensions and deeded compensation

- Veteran's Administration if the individual was receiving Veteran's benefits

- Club and other membership organizations

- Disability insurers if the individual was receiving disability benefits

- Social Security Administration

- Medicare or Medicaid

- Internal Revenue Service for the purpose of obtaining a tax identification number for the estate or trust (or both)

- Utility Companies

- Insurance Companies for real and personal property and vehicles

- Mortgage Companies or Landlord

Finally, consult with legal counsel as soon as possible for further information about what to do next, including other important notifications, determination of beneficiaries, estate administration and distribution of assets.

There are many deadlines that must be met on a timely basis. For example, many states require the Last Will and Testament be filed within a certain number of days after death, and there are deadlines for filing estate tax returns and making tax qualified disclaimers. Your attorney can assist you with all aspects of the estate or trust administration.

After meeting with your attorney you'll have a better idea of what to do and how to do it. Your attorney should instill confidence that estate administration is a process that has a beginning, specific steps in the middle and an end. Be sure to ask how long the process takes in your state, what the costs of administration will be (including filing fees, publication costs and attorneys' fees) as well as what you will be expected to do to assist in carrying out your duties. Be sure to ask how your attorney will communicate with you and how you should communicate with your attorney and their team.

Estate administration doesn't have to be overwhelming. Your trusted advisor team including your attorney, certified public accountant, financial advisors and others should allow you the freedom to delegate many tasks and feel confident everyone is working in your best interest.

CHAPTER TWO

What *Not* To Do When a Loved One Dies

Every man's life ends the same way. It is only the details of how he lived and how he died that distinguish one man from another.

~ Ernest Hemingway

In a book about "what to do" when someone dies, there are inevitably some things you shouldn't do. Don't get discouraged; just be aware of some of the possible pitfalls in the estate administration process.

1. Don't try to do this all by yourself. There are lots of professionals who have been down this road before and have systems and processes in place to help you. This could include attorneys, investment advisors, accountants, appraisers, professional organizers and funeral directors, just to name a few.

2. Don't forget to read the Last Will or Living Trust and any Irrevocable Trusts carefully. These legal documents are ultimately your operating manual and

will provide the directions you need under state law to properly administer your loved one's estate.

3. Don't allow family members to bully or intimidate you into taking actions you don't feel are appropriate or timely. If you are the named fiduciary (executor, personal representative or trustee), then your responsibility is to carry out the instructions left to you by the deceased and to do so properly under state law. Failure to act properly under the law may subject you to personal liability.

4. Don't start distributing assets without guidance from a professional. Be sure the assets you are distributing are going to the correct individuals. One common mistake is agreeing to pay for people to attend the funeral. If they are not named as beneficiaries of the estate, you may be making distributions to individuals who are not entitled to share in the estate assets. You could become personally liable for these expenses. If you do make distributions to an intended beneficiary, then those expenses will become part of their ultimate inheritance.

5. Don't drive the deceased's car while it is still in the name of the decedent. If there is an accident, the estate (as well as the driver) may be liable for damages, and they may not be covered by the deceased's insurance. The better option is to park the car and maintain the insurance until such time as it can be sold or properly distributed.

6. Don't spend your own money for expenses related to the administration of the estate unless you are willing

to do so without reimbursement or until you have evidence that there are plenty of funds to provide future reimbursement.

7. Don't take advice from non-lawyers regarding legal matters. It is not uncommon for non-lawyer friends and family to provide legal advice because they've either been through this before or "they know everything about everything." Only a qualified licensed attorney who has experience in estate administration law should be consulted about the law. This is one time you don't want to be penny-wise and pound-foolish.

8. Don't get discouraged. The estate administration process is just that—a process. It doesn't happen overnight, it takes time and perseverance. It takes patience, a sense of humor and the ability to take on an enormous responsibility in the face of loss and grief. You can do this—get help where you need it.

This is a practical list of things you shouldn't do. It is not all encompassing and shouldn't be the last word on the subject. When in doubt, ask. You aren't expected to know everything there is to know about estate administration. No two administrations are ever the same.

Getting help can make the process smoother and a lot less scary. Staying calm will also help you through the estate administration process. Remember, do not allow yourself to be intimidated by others who think they should be carrying out your role or who think they know more.

All things come to an end, and so will estate administration. Stay focused and organized and you will discover the satisfaction that comes from a job well done.

CHAPTER THREE

What Do I Get and When Do I Get It?

For what is it to die, but to stand in the sun and melt into the wind? And when the Earth has claimed our limbs, then we shall truly dance.

~ Khalil Gibran

"What do I get?" and "When do I get it?" These are two of the most commonly asked questions when someone dies. It seems unfortunate that at a time of loss some people are most concerned about the distribution of the deceased's assets. Sad, but true.

A 96 year old client died recently. When his 92 year old sister, living in a nursing home, was contacted, her first words were, "What do I get?" So you can't say it's generational—it's human nature. Unfortunately, when someone dies, it can become all about the "stuff"—the money, real property, personal property, sentimental items and other items of emotional value—everything that's been accumulated over the course of a lifetime.

Estate administration—whether a trust administration or a probate administration or just attending to the details of asset transfer—all have to happen after someone dies. As mentioned, essentially there are three distinct steps: (1) Identify, gather and value the assets of the estate; (2) identify and pay the legitimate creditors; and (3) distribute the remaining assets to the beneficiaries.

These three steps can be easy or hard, depending on the circumstances, not the least of which is how well family members get along, how efficient the named representatives are in carrying out their duties, and the level of competence and efficiency of the engaged law firm.

For some, the primary goal of the estate administration will be to get their inheritance sooner rather than later. Depending on the circumstances, "sooner" may not be possible. The distribution of assets has to take place in an orderly fashion to ensure each step is properly carried out and one beneficiary doesn't benefit at the expense of another. You also want to ensure that legitimate creditors are properly paid before assets are distributed to beneficiaries. Failure to do so may result in personal liability for you as the fiduciary.

Everyone will be anxious for the administration to proceed immediately. This is common and yet, there are some events that will be out of your control. The administration can't even be commenced until a death certificate has been issued. If there is an error of any kind on the death certificate, this may slow the process. Once the initial administration documents have been properly filed, there are time limitations for family members or others to consent or complain about the pending proceedings.

Then the creditors have to be notified and given their proper notice. Only then will you be in a position to start making distributions.

There are specific, distinct steps to the administration process. Each step is important. If you can persevere and smile, your job will go easier.

CHAPTER FOUR

Probate is Not a Four-Letter Word

It's better to die laughing than to live each moment in fear.

~ Michael Crichton

For some reason, there is a general belief that probate is a four letter word—something to be avoided at all costs. This is inconsistent with the general belief that every person needs a will. When a person has a will as their primary estate planning directive, a probate will generally be required. The only way to administer the terms of a will is with a probate administration.

Part of the reason probate gets a bad name is the process is generally misunderstood. Furthermore, when families fight, it gets blamed on the process rather than the people. Also, some lawyers don't have good office processes and procedures to handle the administration of estates efficiently and effectively. Lastly, there is a perception that probate administration costs too much, takes too long, and is a totally public process.

As a result of the bad rap given to probate, many will attempt to avoid it through the use of joint ownership, beneficiary designations and Living Trusts. Often, more problems are created trying to avoid probate rather than acknowledging that all estates require some administration. It doesn't matter whether it's probate administration or trust administration—the three steps to estate administration are the same.

Step One—Gather and Value Assets

The first step is to identify, gather and value the decedent's assets. This task can be easy or hard depending on how organized a person is. At this stage, important considerations are going to be how the asset was owned—individually, jointly, in trust or with a beneficiary designation. Also important is the value of the asset as of the date of death. This is necessary for determining the initial inventory value of the estate as well as for final tax and estate tax returns. Determining the value of an asset may be as easy as looking at a financial statement, but might require hiring a professional appraiser.

What assets need to be identified? Everything!

This includes real property, personal property, and intangible property. It includes property owned in the decedent's individual name, property owned jointly with others (tenants in common, joint tenants with rights of survivorship and tenants by the entireties), property owned in the name of a trust and property that has one or more designated beneficiaries (either by contract such as a life insurance policy, an annuity or a retirement plan, or by transfer on death or pay on death designations). At the end of your lifetime your estate includes everything you own, everything you control and everything your name is on—in other words, everything!

It's not uncommon for someone to ask, "Well, does the estate include....?" Yes, it includes *everything!*

"Well, how is the Internal Revenue Service (IRS) or Uncle Sam or Aunt Mary or Cousin Sue ever going to know?" It doesn't matter how they will know or find out, it includes everything that has value and belonged to the person who is now deceased. It doesn't include only those things that are convenient or easy to identify, gather and value.

Do you need an appraiser to determine the value of an asset? As mentioned above, perhaps. Ultimately, the answer will depend on the total value of the estate and whether there are items that have significant intrinsic value. An appraisal may also be required if there are family members who might fight over the value of a specific asset. It may also depend on the totality of all the factors taken together, but a good rule of thumb is that everything needs to be valued at its fair market value as of the date of death.

What is fair market value? Is it what you think it is worth? No. Is it what the property tax assessor's office says it is worth? No.

It's the value that a willing seller would pay a willing buyer when neither was compelled to buy or sell and both had all the facts surrounding the purchase and sale. It's the IRS definition of fair market value.[1] It's not just your best guess.

If the asset is a financial asset, like cash, stocks, bonds or mutual funds, getting the value is relatively simple. You can look at the most recent statement provided by the financial institution. If it is a privately held stock or an investment

---

1 http://www.irs.gov/Businesses/Small-Businesses-%26-Self-Employed/
Frequently-Asked-Questions-on-Estate-Taxes#7.

that doesn't have an active market, it may be more difficult to get an accurate valuation and a licensed appraiser may be required. Some assets may receive "discounted" values because of their lack of marketability and lack of control resulting in an overall lower value for estate tax and basis determination purposes.

Whether real or personal property, you can hire a professional appraiser that specializes in the item you need valued. There are specialties for residential real estate, commercial real estate, investment properties, businesses, stocks, coins, jewelry, art and other items of personal property that may hold value. Generally, the valuation date is the date of death, so this is an instance where getting the value determined sooner is better than later.

As you are seeking out the property of the deceased, you might find real property in the form of a primary residence, vacation home or time share; personal property that may include jewelry, automobiles, motorcycles, boats, recreational vehicles, art, and collectibles; intangible property like stocks, bonds, mutual funds, or mortgages; and business interests. You may have to search through a lot of papers to locate all of the assets. Unfortunately, some assets may be harder to find, especially if statements for bank and other accounts are transmitted electronically instead of by mail.

One family was so disorganized they brought in numerous grocery bags full of papers and unopened mail. Years later, undiscovered assets were found through fltreasurehunt.org or other similar websites that can help locate lost financial accounts.

You should immediately establish control over all discovered assets. If the decedent was elderly, be sure to search for cash in unusual places, such as coat pockets and behind pictures in frames and other less obvious places. You will want to look for anything that might be valuable, such as jewelry, art or other collectibles. Once, a client discovered $100,000 cash in the trunk of his grandfather's old car. You may need to place valuables in a safe or other locked storage area. Consider changing the locks to the home to prevent theft or others from helping themselves.

Finally, you may wish to take pictures and complete a simple inventory of items. This will be especially helpful if items do go missing later. If you need help, there are professional organizers and inventory companies that can help you document all the decedent's assets.

An important step in this first step is to maintain insurance on all items that will continue to be in use, such as real property, collectibles, jewelry and other valuables. As for vehicles, if they were in the sole name of the decedent, it is probably best they be taken out of use, but still insured. There's no sense in exposing estate assets to potential liability.

Once you have identified all the property—that is, you have a complete inventory, and you've gotten the fair market value of all of the assets, then and only then are you ready to move on to step two.

Step Two—Pay Expenses, Claims and Taxes

Once assets are gathered and valued, the next step is to pay the expenses of administration, which will include payment of legitimate creditors, final expenses, costs of administration and taxes. Depending on the decedent's state of residence, a probate may be helpful to shorten the time period for creditors to come forward and file their claims. The attorney you are working with can help you understand the laws of your state.

Many people live their lives debt free, except for reoccurring expenses. As a result, they expect that at the time of death there won't be any creditor claims against the assets of their estate. However, you never know for sure what your creditor situation will be when you die. That's because no one can predict all the facts and circumstances under which you might die.

If you've been in an accident, been hospitalized or been in a nursing home, you may have creditors. If you caused the accident that resulted in your death, and especially if others were also injured or killed, you will likely have significant creditors. If you were sick for a long time, you probably have creditors. Certainly the phone company, the electric company and your other utility providers consider themselves to be your creditors—even if you pay them in full each month when the bill is due. The same is true for health care providers and credit card companies—they are all potential creditors of your estate.

You may have other creditors as well. If you've guaranteed a business or personal loan, then you may have creditors you are unaware of. One client who was elderly and not a very good driver ended up with a creditor—someone he had hit in an accident who filed a claim after he died. None of his children were aware of this potential creditor because he never told anyone about the accident.

Creditors have appeared holding hand written promissory notes or IOUs that ultimately end up being legitimate claims that must be paid. If you are in the habit of "loaning" money to friends or children, it's a good idea to document those loans in writing so in the event of unexpected death, your estate can be repaid.

In many states there is a creditor claim period—a statutory period of time when a creditor can file a claim against the estate of a deceased. In some states, the probate process provides a way to shorten this creditor claim period. In Florida, it is possible to reduce a two-year creditor claim period to ninety (90) days simply by opening a probate and notifying both known and unknown creditors.[2]

Known creditors are provided actual notice of their right to file a claim. Unknown creditors are provided notice by publication in the newspaper and an opportunity to file their claim. The shorter the claim period, the better. It's like the part in a wedding when the officiate says, "Speak now or forever hold your peace." Once the creditor claim period has expired, all future claims are barred.

Once the statutory creditor claim period has expired, the estate administrator (a generic term for the more formal, Personal Representative, Executor or Trustee) can have peace of mind knowing all legitimate creditors have been identified and arrangements have been made for full payment, partial payment or objection to the claim.

If a claim is filed that is not legitimate or may be from a valid creditor but in the wrong amount, the estate administrator has the right to timely object to the claim. Upon objection, the claimant will have a statutory number of days to respond to the claim—generally by bringing an independent lawsuit to enforce the claim. Sometimes the parties will agree to an extension of time for the filing of the lawsuit in order to give

---

2 Florida Statutes 733.702.

the claimant more time to ascertain the validity and correct value of their claim. This is common with large hospital bills where all of the insurance payments may not yet have been received and processed.

In our current economic environment, it is not unusual to have an outstanding mortgage balance on a piece of real property greater than the value of the underlying property. Normally, a secured creditor like a mortgage company would not have to file a claim. The value of the property should be more than sufficient to cover the value of their claim.

However, when the property is worth less than the mortgage amount, notice should be given to the mortgage company so they have the opportunity to make a claim against other estate assets. Many times they fail to timely file their claim and as a result, the estate assets are insulated from future claims from the mortgage company. The same may be true for a condominium or homeowner association and others who may have a lien against a property. If the homeowner is in default, the property may still go through foreclosure and the bank (or other creditor) might get the property, but they won't have an additional claim against other estate assets.

If all claims are legitimate, the estate administrator is responsible for payment of the claims from the decedent's assets. What if there aren't enough assets to pay all the claims? This is not unusual. In this event, each state statute generally has a scheme for the priority of claims. Some claims have higher priority than others and must be paid first. Then other, lower priority claims can be paid or pro-rated depending on the amount of the estate assets.[3]

---

3 Florida Statutes 733.707.

There may also be a process for negotiating claims so that all creditors get paid, but not necessarily the full amount. Sometimes, only first priority claims are paid—those to the attorney who handled the administration, those to the certified public accountant who prepared the final tax returns, those to the provider of medical care in the last sixty (60) days and those to the individual who paid the funeral expenses (up to a specified dollar amount). Of course, if there's not enough money or resources to pay the creditors, the beneficiaries are unlikely to receive anything either.

On the other hand, there may be assets that fall into the category of exempt assets. These are assets that may pass to beneficiaries exempt from the claims of creditors. In Florida, this includes your homestead property, two automobiles, household property up to $20,000 in value[4] and any spousal or family allowance (up to $18,000) for qualifying family members.[5]

In some states, assets with beneficiary designations or assets held as joint tenants with rights of survivorship or as tenants by the entireties are also not available to pay creditor claims. Life insurance proceeds and retirement plan benefits may also be exempt from the claims of creditors.

Generally a petition is filed with the court to determine the exempt estate assets. Upon approval, those assets will not be used for payment of creditor claims and may be distributed to the beneficiaries.

Other expenses can include the payment of final expenses, such as medical bills or long term care expenses;

---

4 Florida Statutes 732.402.

5 Florida Statues 732.403.

administration expenses, such as filing fees, legal fees, appraisal fees, accountant fees and fiduciary fees; and taxes, such as state and federal estate taxes and any taxes due on the last income tax return.

In large estates, estate taxes may be due. The estate tax return, a Form 706 is due nine months after the date of death.[6] A good way to remember this date is the saying, "It takes nine months to come into this world and the IRS gives you nine months to pay your estate taxes on the way out." The estate tax exclusion amount and estate tax rates have been changing in recent years. Make sure you understand what the estate tax exclusion is both from a federal and state standpoint. In addition, married decedents may have marital estate exemption and portability options.

Fiduciary and attorney fees may be set by statute depending on the state of administration. Some states, like Florida, have codified a "reasonable" fee for ordinary services.[7] Extraordinary proceedings, like creditor claims or beneficiary disputes, can add thousands of dollars in fees and costs, not to mention the additional time required to resolve the controversy.

It is important you know what to expect in terms of fees and costs. Your legal professional should provide an engagement letter outlining the services that will be covered for the quoted fee and those services that may cost extra.

Once the claims of all creditors have been satisfied, the estate administrator can be confident about the next step—distributing assets to the beneficiaries.

---

6 http://www.irs.gov/Businesses/Small-Businesses-&-Self-Employed/Filing-Estate-and-Gift-Tax-Returns.

7 Florida Statutes 733.6171.

Step Three—Distribution to Beneficiaries

The final step in the estate administration process is what everyone is waiting for—how much do I get and when do I get it? Once all assets are secured, appraised and inventoried, and all expenses are paid, including creditors and taxes, the final step is distribution of the balance of the estate assets to the beneficiaries according to state law, the terms of the Will or the terms of the Trust.

The Will or Trust may also make clear whether the item being distributed will continue to be subject to any attached lien (e.g., mortgage) or if the estate was supposed to pay off the lien before distribution. Absent a specific instruction, the lien will follow the property and become the obligation of the beneficiary.

If distribution is to be on a pro rata basis (e.g., each of three beneficiaries to receive one third), it is important that all beneficiaries be treated fairly and equally. While it is not required that assets be sold for distribution, the beneficiaries may nonetheless agree to liquidate all or some of the assets and simply divide the cash proceeds. This may be especially helpful when beneficiaries will own real property together but may not all get along or may live in different states. Sometimes beneficiaries will want their distributions "in kind", before liquidation, such as in stocks or bonds.

Sometimes there will be ambiguity about the identity of the correct beneficiaries. In this instance, your attorney may petition the court to determine the proper beneficiaries. This is important so the estate administrator doesn't make improper distributions and incur potential personal liability.

What if a beneficiary is a minor child? This happens more frequently than you might expect. When it does happen, a separate legal proceeding—a guardianship—either of the person or the property or both may be required. If the minor child has a biological parent who is living, that person will likely be the natural guardian of the person. However, most states prohibit children under the age of majority from owning assets over a certain dollar amount.

When a minor child becomes the beneficiary of assets, then a guardianship of the property must be initiated for the purpose of placing the minor child's assets under the supervision of the court until the child attains the age of majority. The court will appoint an appropriate guardian of the property (this could also be the child's biological parent), and that person will have the ultimate responsibility for safeguarding the assets during the child's minority. Once the child attains the age of majority (either 18 or 21 in most states), the guardianship will terminate under state law and the assets will be distributed outright to the young adult.

There are many dangers associated with leaving assets to minor children. As a result, clients are counseled to create trusts for minors and vulnerable adults to provide "inheritance protection" that may last for their lifetime.

Bad things can happen to good people. Sometimes when a beneficiary is not mature enough to be responsible for the management of assets, it is referred to as "affluenza"—a not uncommon occurrence that generally results in the spending of a windfall inheritance.

Leaving money outright to a beneficiary will almost always result in the individual spending the entire inheritance within 18 months after receipt. The insurance industry has shown us that it doesn't matter how old a beneficiary is or how much they receive, inherited money is meant to be spent. If you want to ensure your beneficiary has some spending guidance and protection from the claims of creditors (including divorce), then a trust may be a good solution.

If a distribution is to be made to a person who is receiving needs based government benefits (such as a special needs person or an elderly person in a nursing home), there are steps that can be taken to maintain the benefits for that person and also provide for an enhanced life experience. Special needs trusts can protect assets while ensuring ongoing eligibility for government benefits. The creation of a special needs trust should be done only with the assistance of a qualified legal professional with experience in this area of planning.

Sometimes a beneficiary is not an individual, but a continuing trust for the benefit of one or more individuals. In this case, the estate administrator must ensure the assets are properly transferred to and titled in the name of the continuing trust. This process will include obtaining a new tax identification number (TIN) for the trust and establishing an account at a financial institution for the purpose of holding, administering, investing and distributing the trust assets according to the trust instructions.

If the beneficiary is an adult receiving an immediate, outright distribution, the estate administrator will issue a check to that beneficiary in the amount of the specified distribution. Thereafter, what the individual does with the money is not the ongoing responsibility of the estate administrator.

As you can see, there are lots of distribution options. Assets may be distributed outright, distributed periodically, or held in a continuing trust for a beneficiary's lifetime or in some cases, for generations. If assets are held in a continuing trust, the Trustee will be responsible for the administration, investment and distribution of trust assets according to the terms and conditions set forth in the trust document. The Trustee does not have the ability to change the terms of the trust, but instead is required to ensure the trust instructions are followed precisely.

Sometimes assets will not be wholly distributed and some will be withheld for the payment of taxes on a final income or estate tax return. It is important this figure is accurately calculated so a proper amount is withheld for this purpose.

When making a final distribution, it is important for the estate administrator to get a receipt from the beneficiary. The receipt does a couple of things. One, it insures the proper receipt of the money by the beneficiary; and two, it can include language that if there's been a mistake of any kind, the beneficiary will refund the money back to the estate until such time as the mistake is resolved.

Once the assets have been fully distributed, the estate administrator can move toward closing the estate administration. The administration of an estate is complete when the Personal Representative is discharged by the Probate Court or when all of the trust assets have been distributed to the intended beneficiaries, including continuing trusts.

Upon final distribution, the estate will be ready to close. Please see the chapter on "When is Administration Complete?" for more information.

CHAPTER FIVE

It's all About the Documents—The Difference Between Wills and Trusts

A man with outward courage dares to die; a man with inner courage dares to live.

~ Lao Tzu

Good estate administration starts with proper estate planning. Estate planning should focus on pre-planning rather than crisis planning. Without planning, your heirs may be in crisis trying to locate your assets or understand what you want with regard to the distribution of your estate. Your heirs may incur unexpected and significant expenses due to unnecessary administration costs or due to your lack of pre-planning.

One gentlemen died without a will and has so many potential heirs that the estate will have to spend considerable sums of money locating all the heirs, leaving the estate with potentially little value.

There is a cost for pre-planning your estate, but there is also a cost for failing to plan. For now, know that a streamlined estate administration process starts with a proper estate plan.

There's an ongoing debate that centers around estate planning documents—specifically, wills and trusts. Is it better to have a will or is it better to have a trust? Generally, the answer is, "Yes." It's better to have something rather than nothing! When you have done nothing, the state where you live has created an estate plan for you. It's probably not the plan you would have created had you taken the time to plan your estate yourself.

Doesn't it make more sense to do your own planning rather than leaving important decisions to your state Legislature?

Most people say they are never going to die. Win the lottery? Yes. Die? Not ever. This is a lofty goal but not one likely to be accomplished.

Ben Franklin is famous for saying, "There's nothing certain in life except death and taxes." This is true, but with a twist. Death is a certainty—but how, when and where all remain unknown.

Taxes are also a certainty—but how much, if any, on what assets, in what time frame—it all has an air of mystery to it.

If you knew the answers to all these questions in advance, estate planning would be easy. You could spend your last dollar on your last day and take advantage of every opportunity for avoiding or minimizing taxes.

Instead, there is only one certainty in life—CHANGE. As a result, you must be prepared and nimble enough to make adjustments—in your life and in your plans for those changes you don't know about now and can't control later.

There are four important types of change—they are the four "L's."

1. Change in your **Life**
2. Change in the **Law**
3. Change in your **Lawyer**
4. Change in your **Legacy**

Change in Your Life

What kind of change might you experience in your life? This topic could be discussed for hours. There could be a change in your family, your health, your finances, the economy, even in the world. Is your life today different than it was fifty years ago? Twenty years ago? What about ten years ago?

How have you responded to the changes in our life? Did you immediately contact all of your professional advisors including your CPA, your financial advisor and your estate planning attorney to make sure your existing plans were responsive to these changes? If you didn't, then you're completely normal—it's human nature to put off until tomorrow the things you should do today. A study of estate planning clients indicated that on average an estate plan is only updated every 19.6 years![8] Has anything happened in the last twenty years of your life that might have an impact on your estate plan?

A 2009 study reveals that forty nine percent (49%) of Americans have done no estate planning at all![9] Most people put off creating an estate plan and instead leave the

---

8 This study was conducted by the National Network of Estate Planning Attorneys.

9 http://press-room.lawyers.com/2010-will-survey-press-release.html.

distribution of their assets to the whim of their state law. Of those that have done estate planning, probably more than ninety percent (90%) of those are more than five years out of date. Why? Many people believe it's a "one and done"—that it's a "to do" item that now has been checked off the list of life's important things to do.

Unfortunately, because most plans are out of date, it is unlikely the plan is what the decedent wanted or intended. Yet, everyone left behind is powerless to change the plan. For example, one man died with a will that stated he wanted everything to go equally to his son and daughter. Unfortunately, when he died, his son was a joint owner on two of his bank accounts, and he had built his house on property owned by his son. As a result, his daughter received nothing and the man's plan failed him completely.

In another case, a man created a will leaving his entire estate to his girlfriend. However, he failed to keep his plan current and when he died his brother discovered (much to his dismay) that the girlfriend was still the primary beneficiary of the estate. Yet they hadn't been together in more than ten years! In addition, their relationship did not end on good terms. It is unlikely the decedent would have wanted his girlfriend to inherit his entire estate, including his business!

Change in The Law

It won't surprise you to learn that changes in the law occur constantly. Essentially, there are four types of law—federal law, state law, judge-made law and title company law. Every day there is a change in the law that may impact the way you do business, how you protect your family, what taxes you may have to pay and what you can and should do with your assets.

The only way to stay current with changes in the law that might affect your estate plan is to have a strong relationship with a legal professional so you have a line of communication available that will put you on alert in the event of a change. Work with a professional that communicates regularly so you will be kept abreast of changes in the law that may impact your planning.

Change in Your Lawyer

Does this mean you should constantly be changing lawyers? Not necessarily. It asks the question about the competency of your lawyer—what is your lawyer doing to stay abreast of changes in the law and in the management of his or her practice so they can be the best lawyer you can get? What are their credentials? What is their reputation? How are they communicating their expertise and staying informed?

As a young lawyer, I didn't know what I didn't know. I did the best job I could for my clients at that time. Today, I do a much better job because of years of ongoing education and experience. In the future, I'll be doing an even better job.

As a client, you always want to be on the receiving end of changes in your lawyer's level of experience and continuing expertise. Look for someone you feel comfortable with as a person and then ask them what they are doing to stay abreast of changes in the law and how they are improving their knowledge and their client's experience.

Change in Your Legacy

This is the way you want to leave assets for the benefit of those you love. There are a million variations on this theme. No two people are going to want to do exactly the same thing. As a result, no two estate plans will ever be exactly alike. This is another area that can change dramatically.

The legacy you want to leave for your loved ones will be affected not only by your wishes, which may change over time, but also by their behavior and their own life status, which can also change over time. Taking the time to regularly review your legacy decisions and the design of your estate plan is a very important consideration. Sometimes, as a result of changes in relationships with family and friends, a person may become more charitably inclined. Alternatively, planning for pets before family members may become a priority.

As part of an estate planning process, it is important to review your estate plan with your attorney every two to three years to ensure the plan remain consistent with your interests, desires, relationships and the law. If you fail to plan, you might be planning to fail.

The Difference Between Wills and Trusts

Not to digress too much. This chapter is intended to discuss the difference between wills and trusts. So far, it's clear that a custom designed plan, well-conceived and regularly updated with competent legal counsel is important. But, the debate surrounding the wills and trusts dilemma remains unresolved. Hopefully you won't be disappointed but part of the answer to this ongoing debate is, "It depends." Whether a will or a trust will be the right foundational planning directive for you will depend on a number of factors, not the least of which is cost and your desired estate planning outcomes.

A Will, sometimes called a Last Will or Last Will and Testament is a written directive for the purpose of directing your affairs including the administration and distribution of your estate at your death. A Will does nothing during your lifetime. It does, however, become extremely important at the time of your death. Your Will, properly executed, sets forth your wishes and desires for the distribution of your life's worth of asset accumulation. It is important to note, however, that your Will can only control or direct those assets owned in your individual name. It is also important to know that a Will requires probate (a form of estate administration) for the proper distribution of assets.

Your probate estate will be administered by a Personal Representative or Executor, a fiduciary you have named to carry out the three steps of administration.

A Trust, sometimes called a Living Trust or Revocable Trust or *Inter Vivos* Trust, is also a written directive for the purpose of directing your affairs, including the administration and distribution of your estate at your death. In addition, however, a Trust is designed to provide instructions for the efficient administration of your assets during your lifetime while you are alive and well and in the event of your mental disability. Your Trust can establish the terms and conditions for the determination of your disability as well as your personalized instructions for your care and the care of your loved ones. In this regard, a Trust is designed to avoid a potential guardianship.

At death, your Trust will provide for the distribution of your assets, either through outright distributions or in the form of continuing trusts—called Testamentary Trusts. And, not to be too confusing but a Testamentary Trust can also be created in a Will. These Testamentary Trusts are for the purpose of providing continuing instructions for the investment, administration, management and distribution of assets for one or more beneficiaries. As you learned, a Trust can continue for a short period or for a long period of time depending on your concerns. A Trust can be for the benefit of one person or a number of persons. A Trust can also be created for the benefit of a pet.

The person charged with the responsibility of managing trust assets is generally referred to as the Trustee. This can be you during your lifetime and then others—trusted family, friends or corporate trustees in the event of your disability and then at death.

One of the most commonly claimed benefits of a Trust is that it can avoid the probate process and it may result in estate tax savings. Sometimes these claims can be smoke and mirrors because there are a lot of other factors necessary for a Trust to accomplish these goals. To name a few, all assets must be owned in the name of the Trust, the Trust must contain the proper language for estate tax minimization, and the Trust must be properly administered at the time of death. It is not uncommon for one or more of these elements to be missing at the time of administration.

A Trust can avoid guardianship and that may be one of its finest features. If the trustmaker becomes incapacitated during lifetime, a successor disability Trustee can take over the day-to-day management of trust assets without the necessity of a guardianship. Most people want to avoid probate. It's better to avoid a guardianship. A guardianship is the worst kind of lawsuit. It's one your family files against you, you have to pay for it, and ultimately, you lose. In a guardianship, your rights and the ability to make decisions for yourself have been transferred to a person selected by the court. With a Trust you can avoid both the court and you can personally select the individual(s) you choose to administer the trust assets.

A Trust can also avoid the necessity for multiple estate administrations. If you own property in a number of different states, at your death it may be necessary to commence a probate and administer your assets in each of those individual states. Property owned by a Trust will avoid the need for multiple state administrations and can save thousands of dollars in costs as well as significant amounts of time.

Whether you choose a Will or a Trust as your foundational estate planning tool, keep your estate plan relevant by reviewing its terms, confirming the ownership of assets and beneficiary designations and updating the contents every couple of years to make sure you are avoiding the problems that can be created by the four L's. This is the only way to ensure your estate plan will work the way you want, when you need it.

CHAPTER SIX

It's All in a Name—How You Own Your Stuff Is Important

Death is not the greatest loss in life. The greatest loss is what dies inside us while we live.

~ Norman Cousins

How you own your assets affects the transfer of your assets at death. Asset ownership is one of the most misunderstood areas of the law for non-lawyers and can affect estate planning decisions in very important ways.

Few people realize that every time you open a bank or brokerage account, complete a beneficiary designation form or execute a deed, you are engaging in estate planning. As a result, there are lots of well-meaning people giving advice that can have a dramatic impact on your estate planning results and what happens when you become disabled or die.

Most people think of estate planning as simply creating a Will or a Trust. They don't realize that a Will or a Trust is irrelevant unless they own their property in their individual name (for a Will based plan) or in the name of their Trust (for a Trust based plan).

Assets owned with another person as joint tenants with rights of survivorship (JTWROS) pass to the surviving owner upon the death of one owner. Assets with beneficiary designations or pay on death provisions will pass to the named beneficiary at the time of death. Ownership and beneficiary designations can often be at odds with the language of a Will or a Trust. This is why it is important to work with a counseling-based attorney so you can avoid the creation of "competing plans."

Estate planning can involve creating a combination of types of ownership to accomplish your estate planning goals. Consequently, it is important to understand the different types of asset ownership, and that each specific category of ownership controls how an asset is transferred at death.

Without this understanding, you might accidentally be creating estate planning results you don't intend. You might also be creating delays, expenses, creditor claims, taxes or other results for your family and loved ones they didn't expect.

The basic rules regarding how assets are transferred are the same for both married and unmarried couples. However, state laws build in safety nets for married couples, and sometimes for their children, to make sure they are not accidentally disinherited. Unmarried partners have no automatic state protection to avoid disinheritance. As a result, it is essential that unmarried persons create their own safety nets to ensure their wishes will be followed. Asset ownership will be a key feature of making sure assets pass to the proper individuals.

Understanding the rules that control transfers at death is easiest if you remember that each category of ownership has an "instruction sheet" for the disposition of the asset. The instruction sheet might be a Will, a Trust, a beneficiary designation or the terms of a contract.

Operation of Law

States create categories of property ownership that automatically give ownership of the property to the surviving owner(s) at the death of one owner. These types of ownership are either created by the common law of a state or are codified by state statute. For example, tenancy by the entirety (TBE) is a type of ownership with survivorship provisions that is limited to married couples. Probate is not required to determine who receives the property at the owner's death. In addition, there may be important asset protection provisions connected to this type of ownership.

Assets Held Jointly With Others

Assets can be owned with others as tenants in common (TIC) or as joint tenants with rights of survivorship (JTWROS). Most people prefer the JTWROS form of ownership because the asset passes to the joint owner by operation of law at the time of death. However, if you are trying to accomplish ownership objectives as a do-it-yourself project, it is not uncommon to fail to include the required "survivorship" language when executing a deed. As a result, it is possible to believe the asset will pass by survivorship but in reality only a tenancy in common has been created. The difference in ownership determines whether a probate will be required, how the asset will ultimately be owned and whether that asset will be subject to the claims of creditors.

Tenants in Common (TIC)

At death, a person's interest in an asset held as tenants in common is controlled by the individual's Will and passes to those persons named in that instrument. Property held as tenants in common can be in any percentage of ownership from a 99 percent interest to a one percent interest. No matter the percentage, the asset is controlled by your Will (or in the absence of a Will, by state law). The beneficiary under the Will then becomes a joint owner of the asset with the other remaining joint owners—a situation referred to as unintended partners. There is no built-in survivorship language as in a JTWROS owned asset. Assets commonly owned as TIC are real estate and stocks or bonds.

Joint Tenants with Rights of Survivorship (JTWROS)

This form of property ownership is one of the most common examples of the operation of law principle. It is popular because it is easy and inexpensive to create. Many people choose this type of ownership because it avoids probate and appears to create a fair division of assets between couples, married or not. However, these so-called advantages can obscure some of the less desirable qualities of JTWROS, such as:

- During lifetime, joint ownership with rights of survivorship property is subject to the creditors of either owner. If one joint owner has liabilities from a serious accident, a failed business or for some other reason, the jointly held property could be attached to cover the joint owner's debts. This is one of the primary reasons this type of joint ownership of property is not recommended, even for married individuals.

- A taxable gift can be triggered if unmarried owners contribute unequal amounts to the cost of acquiring the asset. When a couple, married or unmarried, buys property and creates a JTWROS form of ownership, in the eyes of the IRS there is a gift to any owner who did not contribute equally toward the cost of acquiring the property.

- For married couples, this gift is a non-taxable event due to the ability of spouses to make unlimited gifts to each other tax free. For unmarried couples, however, unintended gift tax consequences can be triggered. If the portion of the property titled to the non-contributing partner exceeds the Federal annual gift exclusion limit ($14,000 in 2015 and increasing periodically with inflation)[10], there will be an obligation on behalf of the donor/owner to file a gift tax return and report the gift to the IRS. The effect of these lifetime gifts in excess of the annual exclusion limit is a reduction in the amount a person can leave at the time of death without an estate tax obligation.

- The entire value of the asset will be included in the estate (for purposes of calculating the federal gross estate tax) of the first owner to die unless the survivor can produce proof of his or her contributions to the

10 http://www.irs.gov/Businesses/Small-Businesses-&-Self-Employed/ Frequently-Asked-Questions-on-Gift-Taxes#2.

property or other proof as to why less than the full amount should be included. The survivor might want to show less than full ownership by the deceased owner in order to reduce the federal estate tax and state estate tax, if any.

- Structuring financial accounts as joint tenants with rights of survivorship makes the account available to all joint owners and any owner can legally withdraw all of the account funds without the permission of the other owners. Indeed, one of the first instructions divorce attorneys normally give their clients is to immediately remove all assets from joint accounts in order to obtain control over the funds and have the upper hand in negotiations thereafter. Consider, too, that the creditors of any one owner will have access to the account. For unmarried individuals, joint ownership with rights of survivorship may not be a prudent form of ownership.

- There can be income tax consequences to unmarried couples who own property as joint tenants with rights of survivorship. The income tax consequences involve capital gains on property. The cost to acquire a piece of property or an asset is called the "basis." If property is later sold or transferred, the capital gain (or loss) is calculated on the difference between the basis and the sale price or its fair market value on the date of transfer.[11] When a property transfers at the death of the owner by a will or a trust, for example, the tax basis of the property is the fair market value of the

---

11 http://www.irs.gov/Businesses/Small-Businesses-%26-Self-Employed/Cost-Basis-Reporting-FAQs.

property on the date-of-death even if the transfer is actually finalized later. In tax terminology, this is called a "step-up in basis" which means that the recipient of the property acquires a basis in the property equal to the fair market value of the property on the date of the owner's death. Then, when the property is sold, the capital gain is the difference between the value on the date-of-death and the amount for which the property was sold. The recipient isn't required to use the value of the property when the property owner originally acquired the property. Obviously, this can save large sums of money in capital gains taxes.

It is always important to consult with appropriate advisors if your assets are sizeable to be sure you understand the tax consequences of transferring your estate at death.

Joint owners who receive property as a result of rights of survivorship only receive a percentage of the step-up in basis. This percentage correlates with the percentage of each individual's contribution to acquire the property. Married couples are presumed to have contributed 50% each. However, one hundred percent (100%) of joint property will be included in the estate of the first of unmarried partners to die unless the partners can show the actual percentage they contributed to acquire the property.

Other issues to consider with regard to joint ownership:

- A joint owner may require the consent of the other owner to sell real property held as JTWROS during life (this can be a good thing as well—read the section on disadvantages for contract assets below).

- There is no mechanism to hold JTWROS property in trust for the benefit of a disabled surviving joint owner. If the survivor is in a nursing home at the time the other owner passes away, the value of the property might make the survivor ineligible for public benefits based on financial need.

- Joint ownership with rights of survivorship does not work well in the event of the simultaneous death of all owners since the property will be included in the estate of both owners. The second owner will not have time to make alternative plans. In Florida, the law presumes that if all of the joint tenants with right of survivorship die simultaneously, or it is impossible to determine the order of death, each individual is deemed to have owned 50% of the property in their individual name. As a result, the property will thereafter be distributed pursuant to each decedent's will or the state laws of intestacy.

- Federal and state estate taxes may be due at the death of the first owner and the estate might not have sufficient liquid assets to cover the obligation. In addition to gift and estate tax consequences, if an owner, either married or unmarried, is not a U.S. citizen the rules for gift and inheritance taxes may vary. In some states, there may also be a state inheritance or estate tax at the time of death.

- "He who lives the longest wins"—this is one effect of the JTWROS form of ownership. The last person standing is the one who owns the asset. Then the surviving owner can decide who gets the asset—

regardless of the original understanding of the joint owners. Therefore, there is no guarantee the property will go to the people originally agreed upon between the owners.

This can hold particular importance to owners who want to provide for children from prior relationships after the demise of the second owner or where there are concerns the survivor might remarry in the future or be vulnerable to exploitation in subsequent relationships.

There are numerous examples where parents in a second relationship have assured their respective children from prior relationships they will be provided for in the event of their parents' death.

In one case, at the husband's death it was discovered that the bulk of the assets were owned as joint tenants with rights of survivorship with the second wife, or the second wife was named as the beneficiary of life insurance and retirement plans. As a result, the second wife became the sole owner of 100% of the property and she was free to use this property during her lifetime and then distribute it at the time of her death as she might choose. In this case, she made it clear to her husband's children that they were not included in her estate plan. This is an all too common scenario that is repeated daily upon the death of a spouse in a second or more marriage situation.

Transfer on Death Deeds (TOD) or Deeds with a Retained Life Estate or Remainder

These deeds to real estate are individually owned for one or more lifetimes with a survivorship or remainder feature. The asset remains in the individual name of the owner but it is *not* controlled by a will or the probate process because the deed has a built-in survivorship provision that directs who gets the property at the owner's death.

This type of deed is easy and inexpensive to create. At the death of the owner, the survivor merely produces proof of death, and an affidavit is generally filed with the county recorder's office to create a paper trail showing how and why title was transferred.

Transfer on death assets do not have all of the disadvantages that JTWROS property have in terms of potential gift tax issues or being subject to a joint owner's control or creditor's control. However, some disadvantages to transfer on death are as follows:

- The entire value of the asset is included in the deceased owner's gross estate for purposes of calculating the federal and state estate tax.

- If estate taxes are due at the death of the owner, the estate might not have sufficient liquid assets to pay them. This may force the sale of the property to pay the taxes.

- The asset is available to the owner's creditors during life (but not available to the survivor's creditors until the survivor receives the property in his or her own name at the death of the owner.)

- There is no mechanism to hold the asset for the benefit of a disabled survivor.

- The survivor decides who gets the asset once it is transferred to the survivor's name regardless of what the original owner and the survivor discussed prior to the original owner's death.

- This form of ownership may not be available in every state.

Contractual Property Rights

Many people have contracts that allow an asset to pass by beneficiary designation, or in other words, by contract. Some of these contracts are associated with employee benefits at work. The most common examples of assets transferring via contract are life insurance policies, retirement accounts, annuities and payable-on-death accounts.

Payable-on-death provisions might appear to be the same as transfer-on-death deeds. They are not technically the same since they do not get their legal standing from state law but from internal policies created by financial institutions. Therefore, they belong to the family of assets that transfer via contract provisions rather than by operation of law.

Trusts are technically part of this category, but are discussed separately because of their unique features. A Trust can be drafted to overcome many of the disadvantages of other forms of ownership and also provide disability planning opportunities.

The terms of the contract permit the owner to identify who receives the property under the contract when the owner dies. The owner must complete a beneficiary designation form identifying the beneficiary. The beneficiary designation form is the instruction sheet for the proceeds controlled by the contract.

A Will has no power over the contract proceeds and will not direct who gets the benefits under the contract. The only exception to this rule is if the beneficiary designation form is defective for some reason or if the named beneficiary dies before the owner dies and there is no one else named to take the benefit under the contract, or if the owner has named their estate as the beneficiary. In this case, the contract will have an owner (who is deceased) but no named beneficiary. Therefore, probate will be needed to direct who gets the benefit.

Often, disputes arise over the failure to rename beneficiaries when people have entered into new relationships. Generally, the discovery is made that someone from a long ago relationship is still the named beneficiary on a retirement plan or insurance contract. The intended beneficiary is unhappy about the prospect of not receiving the assets and inevitably brings a lawsuit to try and establish their rights. Most of the time, the named beneficiary on the contract prevails. Although some states are attempting to alleviate this issue with respect to divorcing couples, the statutes are generally not failsafe.

Contract assets have some of the advantages of the other ownership methods discussed above:

- There is no need for probate unless there is a problem with the beneficiary designation.

- There are no costs associated with creating the beneficiary designation.

- The transfer process is private and is not part of a court record.

- Some benefits are not considered income to the beneficiary so no income tax is due upon receipt.

- The asset is generally not available to the decedent's creditors, although some states are looking into changing that result.

- A trust can be named as a beneficiary to avoid issues associated with outright distributions.

Some disadvantages of contract assets include:

- The asset is available to the owner's creditors during life (unless exempt under state law) and may be expended by the time of the owner's death.

- The asset will be included in the deceased owner's estate for purposes of calculating the federal and state gross taxable estate.

- There is no mechanism for holding the asset for the survivor's benefit if the survivor is disabled and receiving government benefits at the time of the transfer.

- If a non-spouse is the named beneficiary, the payout schedule for retirement benefits may be less favorable. Generally, a spouse-beneficiary is afforded the opportunity to roll-over a retirement account into his or her name and to continue the income tax deferral during the balance of their lifetime and potentially for the lifetime of their named beneficiaries. A non-spouse does not have this roll-over capability.

- An unmarried owner can change the beneficiary any time prior to death or incapacity without the beneficiary's consent, where married couples may not have the same flexibility to change the beneficiary from the spouse without the spouse's written consent.

A vivid example of how failure to plan and failure to update beneficiary forms can cause emotional and financial hardship for a family is the following case. An unmarried couple failed to properly designate each other on their respective life insurance beneficiary forms. They also failed to do any estate planning, and did not have a Will to provide for each other. When one of the individuals died, it was discovered that the father, not the partner, was the beneficiary on the life insurance policy. Sadly, the father predeceased his son. Therefore, the default language in the son's insurance contract provided that his estate—again, not his partner—was the ultimate beneficiary.

The deceased did not have a Will, so the laws of intestacy (as determined by state law) controlled the disposition of the insurance proceeds. Under the rules of intestate succession his mother was the beneficiary of his entire estate. Unfortunately at the time, his mother was living in a nursing home, was receiving Medicaid and was mentally incapacitated. Her incapacity required the appointment of a guardian to handle the insurance proceeds. It was also necessary to implement a plan to protect her from becoming ineligible for her Medicaid benefits due to the receipt of the insurance proceeds. That's the good news.

The bad news is the surviving girlfriend brought several lawsuits to establish her rights in the home she shared with the decedent (owned by the decedent), the vehicles (owned by the decedent), the life insurance (now paid to his estate) and his retirement plan. All of the litigation, the pain, the family trauma—all of it—could have been avoided had the couple taken the time to meet with an estate planning professional, prepare the proper estate planning directives and examine the ownership of assets and beneficiary designations affecting their assets.

Hopefully you're convinced that how you own your assets is nearly as important as actually having an underlying estate plan consisting of proper legal documents, created with a counseling oriented attorney, regularly updated and fully relevant to your current needs, wants and desires for you and your loved ones.

CHAPTER SEVEN

Avoiding the Morbid Scavenger Hunt

*Organization isn't about perfection; it's about effi-
ciency, reducing stress and clutter, saving time and
money, and improving your overall quality of life.*

~Christina Scalise

Most people are not organized—at least not about their
finances. Most people don't keep a budget, balance their
checkbook or have any idea of their net worth. Some are
afraid to look—if they don't look, maybe it will be better than
they expect. Unfortunately, that's not usually the case!

Unless you have experienced a scavenger hunt after
someone died, you may not realize the importance of making
sure your loved ones know where *all* your assets are. Consider that if your loved ones can't find one or more of your
assets, they won't receive the financial benefit. The cost of not
being organized can be significant. The necessity for a morbid
scavenger hunt will cost your family in terms of emotional
burden, time and lost financial opportunities.

As for the emotional burden, most loved ones would
prefer to spend their time grieving and helping each other

rather than going through papers trying to figure out what and where your assets are. The delay in discovering assets will undoubtedly also delay distribution to your beneficiaries. Can they afford to wait? Finally, what if one or more assets are never located—would your beneficiaries consider that a financial burden?

Today most people have computers. We are encouraged to be "green," to receive all statements and bills electronically. We are discouraged from printing unnecessarily. We all want to do what we can to save our natural resources, and many recognize that going green is an important way to help. As a result, many people do not receive their monthly financial statements in the mail. People also pay their bills online— sometimes through automatic payment and debit programs. If you are trying to consolidate financial information, there are computer programs that can help collect and organize monthly financial information. One example is mint.com.

Since so many of us use computers and receive state- ments and bills electronically, not only do our loved ones have to go through our papers and our mail, but now they may also have to review our email communications (*if* they can access them). How organized are your email communications? In fact, many people don't even save email communications regarding their accounts and bills. So how will your helpers find these assets?!

What if your loved ones never find the $100,000 account you have at an online bank? How will they know where to look if you don't tell them? If your loved ones have access to your password information, this may make the job of identifying and locating your assets easier. If they don't have access to your password information, it might make it harder. As a result, it is a good idea to keep a list of all passwords somewhere safe, but accessible. Otherwise, it may be necessary to hire a computer expert to "hack" into your account to access online financial information.

If you feel you absolutely cannot get yourself organized, ask for help. If you work with a financial advisor, he or she likely has a booklet that can help you get organized. These handbooks are usually designed to ask you all the relevant questions to help you get organized with your assets. Alternatively, ask a trusted family member or friend to help you. If you don't know anyone you can trust, there are accountants and other individuals you can pay to help you get organized financially.

If you like computers, use Excel or Microsoft Word to create your list. If you don't like computers, create your list manually or use a file system. Create a file or index card for each account (bank, savings, certificate of deposit), each retirement account, each pension account, each annuity, each life insurance policy, each business, each real estate property, and each insurance policy on your real estate and vehicles,

Getting organized with your finances is one of the most important gifts you can give your loved ones. When you create your list, include all relevant information. Here are some items that should be included on your list:

- Bank Accounts
- Savings Accounts
- Certificates of Deposits
- Investment Accounts
- Stocks and Bonds

- Mutual Fund Accounts
- Retirement Accounts
- Pension Accounts
- Annuities
- Life Insurance Policies
- Automobiles (with lender information)
- Boats (with lender information)
- Recreational Vehicles (with lender information)
- Real Estate Holdings (with mortgage information)
- Promissory Notes (money owed to you)
- Location of Business Documents
- Location of your Safe Deposit Box and Key
- Valuables (e.g., jewelry, art, collectibles)

In addition, you should include a list of your professional advisors as follows:

- Estate Planning Attorney
- Business Attorney
- Other Attorney(s)
- Accountant
- Financial Advisor(s)
- Tax Preparer
- Clergy

Finally, don't feel you must share this information with your loved ones now. It is only important you tell them where they can find this information in the event you become incapacitated and when you die. Remember, it's not about perfection—it's about helpfulness. Your friends, family and professional advisors will appreciate your organization!

CHAPTER EIGHT

Estate Administration and Taxes

"Death, taxes and childbirth! There's never any convenient time for any of them."

~ *Margaret Mitchell,* Gone with the Wind

Tax considerations are always a concern when conducting an estate administration. There may be the decedent's final personal tax return, income in respect of a decedent, estate income tax returns, trust tax returns, capital gains taxes, property taxes, state estate taxes, federal estate taxes, and generation skipping taxes to consider. The use of a tax qualified disclaimer may be an important tax planning tool. Be sure to consult with a qualified tax advisor to make sure you are getting all the information and advice you need in this area.

The decedent's final tax return will be due on April 15 of the year following the individual's death. A good starting point in the preparation of the final return is to make sure you don't miss anything on prior years' tax returns and have a conversation with the decedent's usual accountant or tax preparer. The Internal Revenue Service is generally a priority creditor so you want to make sure there are sufficient funds reserved to pay taxes prior to making final beneficiary distributions.

Income in respect of a decedent is defined by Investo-pedia as "money that was due to a decedent and will pass through to the recipient or estate as income during that tax year." The recipient (beneficiary) must declare the money as income in respect of a decedent (IRD) for any year in which income is received. The estate must also claim the income, but may claim a deduction in the amount of income tax due on the IRD. Income in respect of a decedent arises when the decedent may have had a last paycheck or unpaid commissions due at the time of death. Tax deferred retirement plans are also another source of IRD income.

If income is earned by the estate or by a trust, there may be an estate income tax return or trust tax return due for each year. Sometimes the income passes through to be taxed at the tax rate of the recipient (beneficiary) and sometimes the tax will be due and payable by the estate or the trust. Although the tax rates for trusts and individuals may be the same, the highest marginal rate is paid on trust income at lower income levels.

Generally when a person dies, the assets they own receive a "step up in basis" so the new basis of the property is the fair market value on the date of death. That new basis becomes the value for determining future capital gains. If the property is sold shortly after death, capital gains may be minimized. If the property is held and sold at a future date when the property has increased in value, the capital gains on the property may be much higher. The tax rate for capital gains can vary with changes in the tax law. As mentioned earlier, if property was gifted during lifetime, the recipient assumes the original tax basis of the donor and may have greater exposure to capital gains taxes.

Property taxes may be due on property owned by the decedent. As the estate administrator it is important to check on the status of property taxes to make sure they are current and to learn when future installments will be due. This is important for the maintenance of the property during the administration phase to avoid penalties or interest that may accrue from delayed or missed payments.

Estate taxes—both state and federal—are of concern anytime someone dies. Under our current federal estate tax system, only decedents with more than $5,430,000 (2015) will have a liability for estate taxes.[12] For married couples, the exemption is $10,860,000 with proper planning and the filing of a timely federal estate tax return (Form 706).[13] The estate tax rate and the lifetime exemption are always subject to change. Be sure you get current information before assuming no estate tax will be due.

In addition, some states impose an estate tax that may start at exemption amounts lower than the federal estate tax exemption. Each state's tax rate will vary. For example, Florida has no state estate tax.[14] By way of example, New York and Massachusetts ("taxachusetts") both have state estate taxes.

Any federal estate tax due will be payable nine months after the date of death.[15] The easy way to remember this rule is you get nine months to come into this world, and nine months

---

12 http://www.irs.gov/Businesses/Small-Businesses-&-Self-Employed/Estate-Tax.

13 http://www.irs.gov/Businesses/Small-Businesses-&-Self-Employed/Estate-Tax.

14 http://dor.myflorida.com/dor/taxes/estate_tax.html.

15 http://www.irs.gov/Businesses/Small-Businesses-&-Self-Employed/Estate-Tax.

to pay the IRS on your way out! The estate tax return is filed on Form 706. You can request an extension for the filing of the return, but the tax is still due. In 2015, the surviving spouse of a decedent was entitled to "carry over" any unused estate tax exemption for use at the time of the surviving spouse's death. In order to preserve this portability right a timely estate tax return must be filed, even if no estate tax is due.[16]

Taxes are an important aspect to the administration of each estate. This is not an area for a do-it-yourself approach because the potential for personal liability is too high.

Generation skipping taxes are another level of tax that may be incurred when a person elects to "skip" a generation with regard to gifting either during lifetime or at death. To skip a generation doesn't mean your children won't benefit from your assets, only that they won't be responsible for payment of any associated estate tax. These estate taxes are deferred to future generations and must be paid upon distribution to the subsequent generations. Currently the generation skipping tax is unified with the estate tax and is currently at $5,430,000 (2015).[17] Again, that number changes regularly and the portability provisions that apply to the estate tax exclusion don't apply for generation skipping taxes.

Planning for generation skipping taxes is a complex area of the law, and consultation with your legal and tax professional is highly recommended.

A disclaimer is the equivalent of a "legal no thank you," and is used in tax planning when an intended recipient of a gift doesn't want or need the gift. The disclaimer allows the gift

---

16 http://www.irs.gov/Businesses/Small-Businesses-&-Self-Employed/Estate-Tax.

17 http://www.irs.gov/uac/Form-706,-United-States-Estate-%28and-Generation-Skipping-Transfer%29-Tax-Return.

to pass to the next intended beneficiary without any gift tax consequences. A tax qualified disclaimer must be executed within 9 months of the date of death and the original recipient can't have accepted any of the benefits.[18] Disclaimers are most often used with life insurance proceeds or retirement plans. They can also be used when proper tax planning has not been done and the less wealthy spouse dies first.

Tax law changes are an example of why estate plans must be updated. Although legal and financial advisors can create directives and build plans to withstand many of the anticipated changes in the law, your best interests are served if your estate plan is subjected to professional scrutiny from time to time.

---

18 http://www.irs.gov/instructions/i709/ch01.html.

CHAPTER NINE

Fiduciary Responsibilities—Attorneys, CPAs, Corporate Trustees and Other Scary People

"The best way to find out if you can trust somebody is to trust them."

~ Ernest Hemingway

First, what is a fiduciary? The term fiduciary refers to a person or organization with a responsibility of care for the assets or rights of another person. The term is derived from the Latin term that means "holding in trust" or "faith." The position requires great confidence, trust, accountability, and a high degree of good faith. In the estate planning arena, a fiduciary could be an agent or attorney-in-fact acting under a financial power of attorney, a guardian or conservator, an executor or personal representative, or a trustee.

Second, what are a fiduciary's duties and responsibilities? A fiduciary has many duties and responsibilities. Following is a list of a fiduciary's important duties and responsibilities:

Duty to read and understand the terms of the trust or will.

Whenever someone is acting in the capacity of an executor or personal representative of a will or trustee of a trust (or both), the will and/or the trust are the operating manual. The first responsibility is to understand and fulfill the duties under the written terms of the will or trust. That is, the responsibility is to do what the deceased instructed in their legal written directives, namely their will or trust, even when the appointed representative doesn't agree or it isn't consistent with what they believe would be correct. The written document is the final set of instructions. These instructions can only be changed by court order.

Duty to comply with the terms of the trust or will and the law relating to trusts or wills.

These duties will depend almost entirely on the language of the trust or will instrument. However, there is an additional requirement to comply with the laws that relate to trusts and wills. Sometimes the written instrument will be contradictory to state law. In this event, state law generally prevails, not the written instrument. Every state has its own set of laws, and as a fiduciary, it is important to know the laws of the state and to seek the advice of qualified legal counsel. If an error is made because the fiduciary is unaware of a legal responsibility, it can result in personal liability as well as removal from the role.

Estate administration is reasonably complex and shouldn't be undertaken without professional guidance. What appears to be simple at first glance may be more complex than initially anticipated. This will be especially true if there are multiple properties, properties in multiple states, business interests, family disharmony, extraordinary creditors, illiquid assets, unpaid taxes or other unexpected obstacles.

Duty to identify and locate estate or trust assets.

Finding personal property may be the easiest to accomplish, as most personal property is kept in the home. Look at insurance policies as well for any insurance coverage that lists valuable items in the deceased's home or that may be kept in a safe deposit box. It is important to make an inventory of personal assets as quickly as possible and lock down the home, just in case others decide to start "borrowing" things!

If the deceased is an elderly person, it is important to check clothing pockets and other places for stashed cash. You might find cash behind a picture in a frame, in a book, or in the freezer. Many people are in the habit of hiding "mad money."

Consider also that the individual may have a home safe or may have a safe deposit box at a bank, so it is important to look for a key or combination. Gaining access to the safe deposit box may prove difficult without a proper court order. However, the safe deposit box may be where you find the person's trust or will and other important documents, such as life insurance policies. It is generally recommended not to keep important documents locked up but easily accessible in the event of emergency.

As for financial assets, most individuals do not make it easy on their fiduciary to find these assets. While it may be very helpful to the fiduciary, most individuals do not even consider that someone will have to locate all their financial assets on their death—or that they might not find them all!

These assets include bank and savings accounts, certificates of deposit, investment accounts, retirement accounts, pension accounts, annuity policies, life insurance policies, deeds to real estate, promissory notes, and titles to motor vehicles, boats and recreational vehicles.

In the typical case, a fiduciary will have to sift through files, papers and mail in order to begin locating assets. However, you still may not find all financial assets, because some people today choose not to receive paper statements for bank, investment and retirement accounts. Rather, they receive their statements electronically via email or they simply log on to their account to review their statements. You may need to review email and other computer files to locate financial assets.

Another possible resource to locate assets is the individual's attorney, accountant and financial advisor.

Duty to control, maintain, preserve and invest estate or trust assets.

One responsibility will be to control, maintain and preserve estate assets. Once assets are identified, it is important to hold or store them in such a way that you will have immediate control over those items. These may include valuable jewelry, art, collectibles, antiques, securities, deeds, titles, promissory notes, cash and anything else you find that you believe may be valuable and especially those items you believe may be subject to "borrowing." Your responsibilities may extend to preserving real estate, maintaining insurance on real property and other valuables, as well as investing estate and trust assets wisely.

It is likely you will be required to obtain an appraisal of real property, business interests and unusual or valuable items of personal property. These appraisals are necessary for the proper valuation of estate assets both for distribution and for tax purposes.

Be careful not to comingle estate or trust assets with your own personal property or assets. Sometimes there is a temptation to do this believing it will be easier to manage. However, you are just asking for trouble.

Duty to exercise the standard of care of a "prudent person."

If you have special skills that might assist you in the estate administration process, because you are an accountant, financial advisor or attorney, you may be held to a higher standard based on your special skills. In any event, you should always strive to act carefully and reasonably, regardless of your background or skills. Again, if you are not familiar with any special responsibilities you may have due to your state's laws, it is important you consult with a qualified legal representative to assist you in this area.

What is a prudent person? A prudent person is one who consistently exhibits good judgment in requesting, reviewing, and weighing information. The concept requires the capacity to quickly and accurately determine that information is adequate for making decisions. A prudent person is attentive, vigilant, cautious, perceptive, and generally governed by common sense and good faith.

Duty of loyalty and impartiality.

Your responsibility as fiduciary is not to consider your interests but the interests of all the beneficiaries as a whole, even if you are one of the beneficiaries. Recall that your responsibility is to follow the terms of the law and the "operating manual"—the will or trust instrument. Your responsibility includes dealing with each beneficiary impartially, not to favor one over the other, and to take great care that you do not appear to be favoring yourself over other beneficiaries, including self-dealing and creating conflicts of interest. If you appear to be favoring yourself over other beneficiaries, it may cause trouble even if you have done nothing wrong.

Duty to avoid conflicts of interest.

You must avoid all transactions between yourself or a third party and the estate or trust that would result in a favorable outcome for you—that is, you must avoid even the appearance of a conflict of interest or impropriety. For example, if you own a business that can provide services to the estate or trust, you should avoid providing those services and seek those services from another vendor. You should also avoid investing estate or trust assets in a business you own or use estate or trust assets to purchase assets you own. You should also avoid co-owning property with the estate or trust.

If a situation arises where a conflict is present, it may be possible to appoint a special independent trustee for the purpose of removing the conflict. When the transaction is complete, the special independent trustee may no longer be required.

Duty to enforce and defend claims against the estate or trust.

If the estate or trust has a claim against another for property or damages, it is the fiduciary's responsibility to enforce that claim. If a claim is made against the estate or trust, either by a creditor of the deceased or by someone who wishes to contest the administration or contest the terms of the will or trust, the fiduciary has the duty to defend these claims. Hiring a legal professional, and possibly an accounting professional to assist in opposing or defending these claims will probably be necessary, but reasonable expenses and fees may be paid out of the trust funds unless the fiduciary's actions become unlawful or involve gross negligence or willful misconduct.

Assess tax implications.

It is likely the fiduciary will need to file the deceased's final income tax return and evaluate whether any state or federal estate taxes or generation skipping transfer taxes are due. A property inventory with appraisals is important here. This evaluation may require a review of any gift tax returns that were filed by the deceased. In 2015, when the estate tax exemption is $5,430,000, most people will not have an estate tax liability. However, there may still be planning options, like portability or disclaimers, you may wish to take advantage of.

As mentioned, any estate tax return is due nine months after the date of death. Even if no estate tax is due, this time frame may be important for the purpose of "portability". Portability gives a surviving spouse the opportunity to "claim" the unused portion of the deceased's estate tax exemption and use it in the future to shelter family assets from the estate tax. There are specific rules that must be followed for portability to be properly used, so make sure you are aware of all of the requirements.

Every state has a different estate tax structure, so it is important to work with legal and accounting professionals on this issue. Working with the deceased's existing trusted professionals may prove to be most beneficial.

Duty to be fair in dealings with, and account to the beneficiaries.

It is always important to act fairly in dealing with both current and future beneficiaries.

One of the first things to understand is the expectations of beneficiaries and any rules the fiduciary may have concerning such things as communication, accountings and meetings. Your expectations and those of the beneficiaries may be completely different.

This includes providing proper information and accountings pursuant to the laws of state in which the estate or trust is being administered. Information may include providing a copy of the trust document to current and future beneficiaries. The fiduciary may be required to provide periodic accountings with information about receipts and disbursements, gains or losses, compensation paid to the fiduciary and other third parties, a list of assets, asset values and liabilities, and anything else required by law.

While it may not always be easy, the fiduciary will have an easier time if emotions are kept under control and procedural formalities are followed. In addition, beneficiaries should always be treated with courtesy and respect. As the fiduciary, you should always respond timely and attempt to deal with disputes as soon as they arise. Open and frequent communication will eliminate possible concerns and distrust from the beneficiaries who do not know or appreciate the scope of the fiduciary's responsibilities.

Additional Tips

Here are some other tips a fiduciary may find helpful:

- Take your role and responsibility seriously.

- Seek professional guidance whenever possible, whether from an attorney, accountant, appraiser, realtor, or other professional advisor.

- Get and stay organized.

- Document all meetings and phone calls, whether with your professional advisors, beneficiaries or third parties.

- Maintain confidentiality of all matters.

- Be civil and courteous with all professionals and with all beneficiaries.

- Keep good records and receipts for expenses you pay from your personal funds and for which you expect reimbursement.

Here are some things *not to do* as a fiduciary:

- Don't procrastinate.

- Don't ignore communications from creditors, professionals or beneficiaries—they will not go away!

- Don't allow yourself to get overwhelmed—get help from a professional if you need it!

- Don't start cashing assets, comingling resources or making loans to anyone.

- Don't allow yourself to be pressured, especially by a beneficiary.

- Don't act alone if you have a co-trustee or co-personal representative.

When it is time to choose your own fiduciary, know this is not necessarily a position of honor—it is hard work with tremendous responsibility and potential personal liability—choose wisely.

The Trustee

I had a friend who died and he
On earth so loved and trusted me
That when this world had set him free
He made me his new Trustee.
He tasked me through my natural life
To guard the interest of his wife;
To see that everything was done
Both for his daughter and his son.
I have his money to invest,
And though I try my level best
To do that wisely, I'm advised
My judgment oft is criticized.
His widow, once so calm and meek,
Comes hot with rage, three times a week
And rails at me because I must
To keep my oath, appear unjust.
His children hate the sight of me,
Although their friend I've tried to be
And every relative declares
I interfere with his affairs.
Now when I die I'll never ask
A friend to carry such a task,
I'll spare him all such agony
And name a corporate trustee.
~ Author Unknown

CHAPTER TEN

When is Administration Complete?

*It is foolish and wrong to mourn the men who died.
Rather we should thank God that such men lived.*

~ *George S. Patton, Jr.*

The completion of administration is usually dictated by someone else. In a probate administration, it's generally the decision of the Probate Court. Once the Court is satisfied all creditors and administrative expenses and taxes are paid and all beneficiaries have received their proper inheritance, the Court will enter an order of discharge or something similar to conclude the probate administration. Upon discharge, the estate administrator is free from further responsibility and personal liability.

The completion of a trust administration is dependent on the terms of the trust—it's generally the Trustmaker who determines when a trust administration is complete. As with a probate, all creditors and administrative expenses and taxes must be paid (and an IRS tax closing letter received if the estate was taxable). However, the distribution to the beneficiaries could take one of a variety of forms.

First, the beneficiaries may receive their distribution outright. Some beneficiaries may receive their distributions at different ages or stages of their lives. The trust may identify certain conditions that must occur before the trust administration is complete. The trust may hold the beneficiaries' assets for a lifetime, protecting the assets and the beneficiary from creditors and predators (including the possibility of a soon-to-be ex-spouse) and, of course, the beneficiaries themselves. In some cases, the trust instrument may allow a trustee to terminate the trust if the cost of administration becomes too expensive and the costs of maintaining the trust outweigh the ongoing benefits.

Whether you have a probate administration, trust administration or both, choose an attorney and other advisors who are experienced in these matters and who will provide you with advice as to all your options. Your trusted advisors should discuss the following items with you:

- Advice regarding the terms and language of the will or trust.

- Advice regarding the law as it is applied to wills and trusts.

- Advice regarding the duties and responsibilities of the estate administrator.

- Advice regarding the notices required by law to be sent by the estate administrator to creditors and beneficiaries.

- Advice regarding the investments permitted in an estate or trust.

- Advice regarding appraisals, selling assets, paying taxes and when to make distributions to beneficiaries.

- Advice regarding the proper use of tax elections and disclaimers.

- Advice for non-U.S. citizen spouses.

- Advice for handling disputes among beneficiaries or between beneficiaries, creditors and the estate administrator.

CHAPTER ELEVEN

Why Prearrange Your Memorial Service?

Ancient Egyptians believed that upon death they would be asked two questions and their answers would determine whether they could continue their journey in the afterlife. The first question was, "Did you bring joy?" The second was, "Did you find joy?"

~ Leo Buscaglia

Many people believe when they provide direction in their will that they wish to be cremated or buried, their family will honor their wishes. In many states, however, the body of a deceased belongs to the heirs, and they can do as they wish. What if your children don't believe in cremation but you want to be cremated? What if they want to save money by cremation but your desire is to be buried?

One way to increase the likelihood that your wishes will be followed is to prearrange your funeral and memorial. You can arrange in advance for your cremation or burial and pay in full for these arrangements. If your children or other loved ones don't agree with your wishes, now they will have to pay *more* money to do what they wish, thereby depleting their ultimate inheritance. Frankly, in this event, they may think twice before changing your prearrangements. So, if you want what you want, and you think there's a possibility someone might disagree, it may be wise to make your arrangements ahead of time.

There are other advantages as well. Usually the cost of a funeral is less if you plan for it ahead of time, and there may also be payment plan options. Even making your arrangements five years ahead of time can make a significant difference in price. Of course, you never know when you'll die, so the sooner you get started, the better.

In addition, preplanning removes a significant burden from your loved ones and can reduce the cost to them in other ways. Often, when families are left with the responsibility for the arrangement of a burial or cremation of a loved one, this act may be one of the last ways for them to express their love. As a result, it is possible to significantly overspend in their effort to show their love, one more time. If a cremation is chosen, loved ones may prefer to use a more expensive cremation casket or remembrance urn. In a burial, loved ones may overspend on items such as burial caskets, headstones, flowers, and other additional items that are nice, but can simply add to the cost.

Making your own prearrangements will give you peace of mind knowing you have removed the burden from your children or other loved ones. In addition, you will have the disposition you want and your loved ones will not overspend. You have the chance to make a logical decision about your arrangements and remove a burden from your loved ones.

Finally, one long term care asset protection strategy when facing a long-term nursing home stay and the possibility of applying for Medicaid is paying for final disposition in advance. Prepaid funeral arrangements are considered an exempt resource from a Medicaid perspective if the contract is irrevocable. This way, not only is preplanning an acceptable way to "spend down" an estate, it completely removes the cost burden from family members in the future when all of the assets have been depleted.

Here are some things to consider when you are making your prearrangements. It is important your family know your wishes, especially if you believe they will honor your wishes. If you think your family may not agree with your prearrangements, consider writing a letter to your loved ones and place it with your estate planning documents so they will have the opportunity to "hear from you" regarding your final wishes.

Cremation

Will you choose an urn for burial or remembrance or do you want your ashes scattered? If you want your ashes scattered, do you know where and by whom? Do you have any special requests?

Traditional Burial

Have you chosen a burial plot and paid for it? If so, make sure your family knows where your plot is located. Do you have a preference as to your burial clothing? What type of casket would you like? Do you want an open or closed casket viewing?

Mausoleum

If you want to be interred in a mausoleum, have you chosen the location and paid for it? Will it be intended for use by other family members? Make sure your family knows where it is located.

Funeral and Memorial Service

Do you have specific requests with regard to the funeral or memorial service? Are you comfortable with your family making these decisions during a time of grief? Some people may want a more solemn event while others may prefer something more celebratory in nature. What are your wishes?

Faith

Are you a member of a particular faith? Have you chosen where you would like your memorial service to be conducted? Is there a specific person you'd like to conduct your service?

Miscellaneous items you may wish to choose:

- Clergy
- Flowers
- Where to send donations in lieu of flowers
- Pallbearers
- Military Honors
- Music
- Prayers, special requests or special readings
- Gathering after the service

- What you want your headstone to read

- What you want your obituary to say

- What you want to be remembered for

- What do you want to say to your loved ones? Here are some examples: *I'd like this event to be more of a celebration . . ."* or *"I want each of you to know how highly I thought of you . . ."* or *"Please remember my favorite charity . . ."*

These are just a few things you can consider as you think about the preplanning of your final arrangements. Your local funeral home or crematorium can give you additional guidance and ideas.

CHAPTER TWELVE

Living Too Long, Dying Too Soon

I'm not afraid of death; I just don't want to be there when it happens.

~ Woody Allen

One thing in life is certain, at some point we are all going to die. Generally the biggest issue is you don't know when, where or how. As a result, it is imperative to plan for yourself and your family in such a way as if you were planning for the worst. That way, you can always hope for the best.

Dying too soon can mean leaving your family or loved ones without the financial security they need to live the lifestyle they have come to enjoy or rely on. There are lots of things you can do to provide adequate protection for your loved ones. Living within your means is one. It means not incurring substantial debt that can't be paid off within a realistic period of time or with the income you have today. It also means having a six-month cushion of expenses in case a tragedy prevents the primary wage earner from going to work every day. It means having disability insurance to pay the bills when a person can't work due to an unexpected disability. It also means having sufficient life insurance to meet the long terms needs of your loved ones so they don't have to change their standard of living or compromise family goals in the event of a premature death.

These issues are important within the context of a book about what to do when someone dies because if these issues have not been properly addressed during your lifetime, they can spell disaster for your loved ones when you die, especially if you die unexpectedly and without warning. As a nation, we are a very optimistic people. We say, "*When* I win the lottery and *if* I die," as if the former is a given event and the other only a slim possibility.

Consider the plight of a widow whose husband died, leaving her destitute. The widow's financial advisor seemed stunned on two fronts; one that the woman's husband had not properly provided for her and two, the woman seemed to take no responsibility for her current predicament. The widow had never participated in family financial decision making, simply leaving all important decisions to her husband. As a result, he had no life insurance, no savings, a mortgage she was unable to pay and he had selected a retirement annuity option that ended at his death. Now she is forced to live on his social security income as her sole source of support. She will have to sell her home in a difficult real estate market, perhaps costing her tens of thousands of dollars in potential retirement savings. Literally, she has no savings at a time of her life when her earning capacity is diminished.

This is not an entirely uncommon occurrence. Far too often financial devastation is experienced by remaining family members, both women and men, when their spouse or partner dies and their financial plan never contemplated the possibility of a premature death. Bottom line, you have to take responsibility for becoming educated about your financial and estate planning options.

There is no shortage of information and advice available. There are scores of talented advisors who would love to do nothing more than educate you about all the ways to create protections for the people you love. There is just no excuse to be uneducated in the areas of financial planning and estate planning.

What about living too long? Is that a possibility? In theory, of course not. We all want to live as long as possible. However, what if you aren't really living, but simply existing? The nursing homes in our country are full of people who, if asked, would probably say they had "lived too long." Quantity of life does not necessarily indicate a life's quality.

One of the best books available on the subject of quality of life toward the end of life is "The Best Care Possible" by Ira Byock, M.D. Dr. Byock is a palliative care doctor dedicated to improving end of life care. He encourages everyone to examine the quality of the last months, weeks, and days of our lives and to demand the best care possible. This is not the care that will necessarily prolong life but will instead make the last days as pain and anxiety free as possible so those last precious moments can be in the presence of the people and things you care about most. If desired, a person can choose to die at home, surrounded by family, friends and pets, without medical intervention intended to only prolong the inevitable.

Living too long might also mean utilizing family financial and emotional resources in a way that takes a significant toll on survivors and caregivers. Many people are terrified by the prospect of what their future might hold if all the family financial resources are required for the long term home care or nursing home care of a loved one. Caregivers can become emotionally and physically exhausted by the daily demands of caring 24-7 for an ill loved one.

Many families are unaware of the resources available to provide assistance with long term care costs. Most feel strongly they would never want a family member to go to a nursing home.

Yet, the reality today is that one out of every two people will need some form of long term care in their lifetime.[19] As our society ages and people are living longer, this number could go even higher. People over the age of 100 are one of the fastest growing age groups in our country.[20] What does this mean for the demands that will be put on already over-worked and underpaid family caregivers and other medical professionals? Will there be enough facilities to provide care for everyone who needs it? Will the Social Security, Medicare and Medicaid programs be able to withstand the increasing demands required for quality care for our aging nation?

Already, all government entitlement programs are under scrutiny and daily attack. What will become of them in the future? We all have to take responsibility for providing for the inevitability that there may be a future need for long term care. You can save for it, insure against the rising cost, but will it

---

19 http://longtermcare.gov/the-basics/how-much-care-will-you-need/.

20 https://www.census.gov/newsroom/releases/archives/aging_population/cb11-194.html.

be enough? Likely, the answer is no, mostly because, as a general rule no one plans perfectly for tomorrow. Instead, we all wait until there's a crisis and then scramble around to find the professionals and resources necessary to meet our current need.

Long term care insurance is the best defense against the rising cost of long term care; but will you get it when you are young and healthy enough to afford it from a company who will still be there when you need it? Let's hope so. If not, then there will still be professionals specializing in the field of elder care and elder law to help you navigate your new found long term care situation.

A book on what to do when someone dies would not be complete without a discussion about what to do before someone dies, when you are face to face with either your own mortality or the mortality of a loved one. Start planning as early as you can. Be aware that planning is a process that takes a lifetime and isn't a one-time event. Prior proper planning will insure a different and better outcome for those you love.

Love begins by taking care
of the closest ones –
the ones at home.
~ Mother Teresa

CHAPTER THIRTEEN

Your Estate Planning Strategy

I had an inheritance from my father,
It was the moon and the sun.
And though I roam all over the world,
The spending of it's never done."

~ Earnest Hemingway

When a person seeks out an estate planning attorney to create their estate plan, sometimes that person knows exactly what they want. Sometimes they believe an estate plan is just about having a will. Sometimes they want to avoid probate, so they believe they want a trust. An estate plan is much more than just having a will or a trust.

A proper estate plan is one that will allow you to remain in control of your assets while you are alive and well, allow you to protect yourself and your loved ones in the event you become mentally incapacitated, and leave what you have, to whom you want, when you want, the way you want, all while also sharing your personal values and life lessons. You can learn more about creating an estate plan that works by reading "What's The Deal With…Estate Planning."

Your estate planning strategy should begin with a search for an experienced attorney who will talk with you about your family, your estate planning goals and how to integrate your assets properly. Your attorney should explore the hopes and fears you have for your family, and counsel you on the options you have to protect yourself and your family. Nothing should be sacred between you and your attorney. You should feel free to share with your attorney everything that concerns you about your situation.

Everyone's situation is unique. If you had to design an estate plan for your neighbor, would you be able to do it? Is your neighbor single or married? Is this a first or second marriage? Is their spouse a non-U.S. citizen? What about their children—no children, lots of children, adopted children or stepchildren? Do they have a special needs family member? How about an elderly parent? Do they have pets they want to plan for? What are their financial resources—are they well off or struggling to make ends meet? Chances are, you probably don't know your neighbor well enough to answer all these questions. There are many things to consider when creating an estate plan. An experienced attorney can help you understand all that is important to you and then assist in the creation of a plan to meet those needs.

There are three key things that must be in place for your estate plan to work as intended:

Proper Asset Ownership

Failure to understand asset ownership and how asset ownership will affect the dispositive provisions in a will or a trust can be fatal to an estate plan. For example, a person might go to an attorney and ask for a will leaving all assets equally to her four children. However, if she owns property jointly with one of her kids or has a beneficiary designation on an account or life insurance naming another child, her plan may not be successful—it will not accomplish her stated goal of leaving assets equally to her four children.

It is not uncommon to see a person, especially among the elderly, to put a child's name on the deed to their home or other property (hoping to avoid probate) or on an account (for convenience purposes for an unexpected event). However, most of the time, the child holding the joint interest in the real estate or account will become the sole owner of that property upon the parent's death, probably an unintended result if the person has other children. What is left is an unequal distribution of assets for the remaining children, completely contrary to the person's intent.

Part of having an effective estate plan is revealing to an experienced estate planning attorney all your assets, how your assets are titled and who has been named as beneficiary of your bank and retirement accounts, life insurance and any other assets you have with beneficiary designations. Only when your attorney understands how your assets are owned will he or she be able to advise you on how to achieve an estate plan that works the way you want it to work.

Sometimes people believe a will controls all their assets. However, nothing could be further from the truth. The only asset a will controls are those assets that are individually owned and have no beneficiary designation. If you own property jointly with your sister, your will won't control that asset.

If you put your son's name on your checking account because he's the child who lives nearby and will be able to pay your bills should you go in the hospital, your will or trust won't control that asset either. If you have life insurance and you have named only three of your four children (because after your fourth child was born, you completely forgot about changing the beneficiaries), your will won't control that asset, and your fourth child will simply be left out.

If you own a home in your individual name, your will controls that asset. If your checking account is in your name alone and has no beneficiary designation, your will controls that asset. While convenience or avoiding probate may be your goal, you can wreak havoc on your estate plan and your loved ones if you don't understand ownership and beneficiary designations. Please read the chapter "Probate is Not a Four Letter Word" to help you understand that probate has its place and can benefit the administration of your estate.

Finally, if you have a trust, it is important that assets be properly titled in the name of your trust in order for your trust to be effective and control that asset. Assets individually owned and not funded (re-titled) into the name of your trust will likely require probate and then be funded into your trust via provisions in your will.

Your best plan is one you design based on your circumstances and your family, but it's best if you work with an experienced estate planning attorney to ensure that the plan you want *actually works!*

Control of the Process

Part of having an effective estate plan is maintaining control over your assets while you are alive and well. Another part is maintaining control of the process should you become incapacitated and after your death.

While you are alive and well, it is important you name someone who can take over the management of your finances and your property should you become mentally incapacitated and are no longer able to manage your own affairs. In the ideal scenario, you will name a "disability trustee" in your trust to step in as successor trustee if you become mentally incapacitated. That person is sometimes the same trustee you would also name to take over as successor trustee after your death.

The next question is who will train your successor trustees in the event you should become mentally incapacitated and after your death? Part of the education of your trustee includes providing that person with an understanding of the following:

- How a living trust works (especially while you are mentally incapacitated), and how to read and understand your trust.

- Your trustee's fiduciary duties—first to you and then to your heirs.

- Important "Do's and Don'ts", such as do seek guidance and advice, get and stay organized, maintain confidentiality of the trust; and don't procrastinate, ignore communications or comingle trust funds.

- How to work successfully with beneficiaries.

- A Trustee's overall duties and powers.

- How to invest assets and maintain proper records.

- What to do about income, gift and estate taxes.

Keep Your Plan Relevant

Once your estate plan is in place, it's important you keep it relevant to your current situation. Don't wait 20 years to update it.

Three things are always changing in your life—your relationships, what you own and the legacy you plan to leave. People are born, get married, divorce, die, and move away. You purchase a home, some rental properties or a vacation home. You might acquire jewelry and valuable art or other collectibles. You may no longer trust or feel you can rely on the people you initially chose to be your attorney-in-fact, personal representative or successor trustee. You may believe providing for your grandchildren or a charity is more important than leaving assets to your children.

The law is constantly changing as well. If you died without a will today, do you know how your assets would be distributed under your state law? Florida recently changed its law regarding spouses and descendants. Has your state law changed recently?

The death of Thomas Kinkade, famous as the "Painter of Light," died in 2012 at age 54. His story is a good example of what can go wrong. .

Thomas Kinkade had been separated from his wife for two years and his divorce case had not yet been settled. Mr. Kinkade had a girlfriend he lived with for eighteen months whom he reportedly planned to marry when his divorce was final. Thomas Kinkade did not have a *current* estate plan. His old will devised his assets to his estranged wife, and although he tried to make two new handwritten wills, the Probate Court found both attempted handwritten wills to be invalid. Both handwritten wills left his assets to his live-in girlfriend.

Mr. Kinkade did not keep his estate plan "relevant" to his current situation. As a result, his estranged wife will inherit his assets. His wife also sued his girlfriend to prevent her from talking to the press.

While Thomas Kinkade surely never thought he would die at age 54, it is a valuable lesson that death or incapacity can happen to anyone, at any time. When Thomas Kinkade first separated from his wife, he should have immediately gone to an experienced estate planning attorney to have his estate plan updated so it reflected his wishes within the confines of the law.

Everyone should review their will and/or trust at periodically, at least every two to three years to make sure it is still relevant. If even one thing has changed in your life, your health or your legacy, don't wait. If the law has changed, don't wait. If you have questions about your estate plan, don't wait.

Your estate planning strategy should embrace the idea that the only thing in life that's certain is—change.

It's never too early to plan,
But you never know when it's going to be too late.

APPENDIX A

Glossary of Estate Planning Terms

Administrator: Person named in your will and appointed by the court to administer your probate estate. Also called an Executor or Personal Representative.

Agent: An individual named in a power of attorney with authority to act on the power giver's behalf. Has a fiduciary responsibility to the power giver. Sometimes called Attorney-in-Fact.

Ancillary Administration: An additional probate in another state. Typically required when you own assets or real estate in a state other than the state where you live that is not titled in the name of your trust or in the name of a joint owner with rights of survivorship.

Applicable Exclusion Amount: The amount of property owned by a decedent effectively exempt from the federal estate and gift tax ($5,340,000 in 2014).

Attorney-in-Fact: An individual named in a power of attorney with authority to act on the power giver's behalf. Has a fiduciary responsibility to the power giver. Sometimes called an Agent.

Basis: What you paid for an asset. Value used to determine gain or loss for capital gains and income tax purposes.

Beneficiary: The person named in a will or trust to receive or benefit from property owned by the maker of the Will or grantor of a Trust. During lifetime, a trust grantor may be a beneficiary.

Buy-Sell Agreement: A written agreement between co-owners of a business to determine the rights of the owners in the event of retirement, termination, bankruptcy, divorce, disability or death.

Capacity: The legal competence to effectively perform a given act (e.g., to write a Will or Trust or enter into a binding contract).

Co-Trustees: Two or more individuals who have been named to act together in managing a trust's assets. A Corporate Trustee can also be a Co-Trustee.

Corporate Trustee: An institution, such as a bank, trust company, or charitable organization that specializes in managing or administering trusts.

Decedent: A person who has died.

Disclaim: To refuse to accept a gift or inheritance so it may be transferred to the next recipient in line. Currently must be done within nine months of the date-of-death to be tax qualified. Sometimes referred to as a "legal no thank you."

Durable Power of Attorney for Financial Matters: A legal directive that gives another person full or limited legal authority to make legal, financial and property decisions on your behalf. May be effective immediately or "springing" depending on your jurisdiction. Valid through mental incapacity or disability. Ends upon revocation, adjudication of incapacity, or death.

Durable Power of Attorney for Healthcare: A legal directive that gives another person legal authority to make health care decisions for you if you are unable to make them for yourself. Also called Healthcare Proxy, Healthcare Surrogate or Medical Power of Attorney.

Estate Administration: The process of settling either a probate estate or trust estate. There are generally three steps that include identifying, gathering and valuing the assets, paying the debts of the estate and distributing the balance to the beneficiaries.

Executor/Executrix: The person nominated in a Will and thereafter appointed by the Probate Court to manage and distribute a decedent's estate in accordance with the terms of the Will. Also known as a Personal Representative.

Fiduciary: Person or entity having the legal duty to act for another person's benefit and occupying a position of trust and accountability. Requires great confidence, trust, and a high degree of good faith. Usually associated with a Trustee, Personal Representative, Executor, Guardian, or Conservator.

Funding: The process of re-titling and transferring assets to your Living Trust. Also includes the re-designation of beneficiaries to include your Living Trust as a beneficiary. Sometimes called asset integration.

Generation Skipping Transfer (GST) Tax: A federal tax imposed on certain transfers, either by gift during life or at death, between a donor/decedent and a person more than one generation removed (e.g., a grandchild).

Gift Tax: Federal tax on completed lifetime gifts made from one person to another. The current lifetime exclusion amount is $5,340,000 for 2014. The current annual exclusion amount is $14,000. May require tax reporting to the IRS on Form 709, a gift tax return.

Grantor: The person who establishes a trust. Also referred to as the "Trustor," "Trustmaker" or "Settlor."

Gross Estate: The total value, for estate tax purposes, of everything one has an ownership interest at the time of death. Includes everything you own, everything you control and everything your name is on.

Guardian: an individual or professional appointed by the Guardianship Court to be responsible for the person or property of a Ward.

Guardianship: A court supervised proceeding whereby after evaluation and review a Guardian is appointed to act on behalf of a minor or incapacitated person (the Ward). A Guardian must be appointed if the incapacitated person did not designate an agent or surrogate in a Durable Power of Attorney (for financial and health care matters) while he or she was competent.

Heir: The person entitled to distribution of an asset or property interest under applicable state law in the absence of a Will. The terms "heir" and "beneficiary" are not synonymous.

Health Care Proxy: A legal document that gives another person legal authority to make health care decisions for you if you are unable to make them for yourself. Also called Durable Power of Attorney for Healthcare, Healthcare Surrogate or Medical Power of Attorney.

Inter vivos: Latin term that means "between the living." An *inter vivos* trust is created while you are living instead of after you die. A Revocable Living Trust is an *inter vivos* trust.

Intestate/Intestacy: When a person dies without a valid will, his or her estate is distributed pursuant to state intestacy laws.

Irrevocable Life Insurance Trust (ILIT): An irrevocable trust for the purpose of holding title to life insurance. Used as an advance planning technique to remove the death benefit proceeds of a life insurance policy from an insured's gross taxable estate. Can be used to take advantage of annual exclusion gifts.

Irrevocable Trust: A trust that cannot be changed, amended or canceled once it is created. Opposite of a Revocable Living Trust created during lifetime.

Intestate: Dying without a Will.

Joint Ownership: When two or more persons own the same asset, either as tenants in common or as joint tenants with right of survivorship.

Joint Tenants with Right of Survivorship: A form of joint ownership where the deceased owner's share automatically and immediately transfers to the surviving joint tenant(s) or owner(s).

Living Trust: A legal entity created during your life, to which you transfer ownership of your assets. Contains your instructions to control and manage your assets while you are alive and well, plan for you and your loved ones in the event of your mental disability and give what you have, to whom you want, when you want, the way you want at your death. Avoids guardianship of property and avoids probate only if fully funded at incapacity and/or death. Also called a Revocable Inter Vivos Trust.

Life Alliance Agreement: A written agreement between two life partners for the purpose of establishing ownership to property, rights and obligations with regard to property and disposition of property in the event of the termination of the relationship.

Life Alliance Partner: A life partner of the same or opposite-sex in a committed, but unmarried, relationship.

Limited Liability Company (LLC): A form of legal entity that can provide limited liability from the claims of creditors. Can be taxed as a sole proprietorship, partnership, s-corporation or c-corporation.

Living Will: A legal document that sets forth your end of life wishes regarding the termination of life-prolonging procedures (respiration, hydration, nutrition) if you are mentally incapacitated and your illness or injury is expected to result in your death.

Personal Representative: Another name for an Executor or Administrator.

Pet Trust: A special trust prepared to ensure your pet receives proper care after you die or in the event you become incapacitated. Contains sufficient funds and instructions to provide lifetime care for your pet. Also names pet caregivers, an Animal Care Panel and Trustees.

Pour Over Will: An abbreviated Will used with a Living Trust. It sets forth your instructions regarding guardianship of minor children and the transfer (pour over) of all assets owned in your individual name (probate assets) to your Living Trust.

Power of Attorney: A legal directive that gives another person legal authority to act on your behalf for a stated purpose. Ends at revocation, incapacity (unless it is a durable power of attorney) or death.

Probate: The legal process of validating a Will, paying debts, and distributing assets after death. Generally requires the services of a qualified attorney.

Probate Estate: The assets owned in your individual name at death (or assets with beneficiary designations payable to your estate). Does not include assets owned as joint tenants with rights of survivorship, pay-on-death accounts, transfer-on-death designations, insurance payable to a named beneficiary or trust, and other assets with beneficiary designations.

Probate Fees: Legal, Executor/Personal Representative, court, and appraisal fees for an estate that requires probate. Probate fees are paid from assets in the estate before the assets are fully distributed to the heirs or beneficiaries.

Revocable Living Trust: Another name for a Living Trust.

Spendthrift Clause: Protects assets in a Trust from a beneficiary's creditors. Prohibits a beneficiary from pledging or borrowing against trust assets.

Successor Trustee: Person or institution named in a trust instrument that will assume responsibility in the event the acting Trustee dies, resigns or otherwise becomes unable to act.

Tangible Personal Property: Personal property that ordinarily has no registered owner, such as furniture, clothing, jewelry, antiques, collections, etc., but not cash or other financial assets.

Tenancy by the Entirety (TBE): A form of joint ownership of property available only to married couples. Very similar to joint tenants with rights of survivorship whereby title to the property automatically vests in the surviving spouse. TBE ownership provides creditor protection in some states.

Tenants in Common (TIC): A form of joint ownership whereby a deceased tenant's share passes to his or her heirs or beneficiaries through his or her estate.

Testamentary Trust: A trust created in a Will or Trust. Only becomes effective at death. May not avoid probate when created in a Will.

Testate: An estate where the decedent died with a valid Will.

Trust Administration: The legal process required to administer trust assets after incapacity or death. Includes the management of trust assets for the named beneficiaries, the payment of debts, taxes or other expenses and the distribution of assets to beneficiaries according to the trust instructions. Generally requires the assistance of an attorney.

Trustee: Person, institution or charitable organization who manages and distributes another's assets according to the instructions in the trust instrument.

Will (or Last Will & Testament): A written document with instructions for disposing of assets after death and appointing a guardian for a minor child. A Will can only be enforced through the probate court.

Resources

The internet provides access to a vast amount of information. Sorting through what's important and discovering what is relevant for you can be overwhelming. Here are some additional resources to answer your questions.

The Law Offices of Hoyt & Bryan, Oviedo, Florida - HoytBryan.com

All of the following books are also available on Amazon.com:

All My Children Wear Fur Coats – How to Leave a Legacy for Your Pet – LegacyForYourPet.com

Special People, Special Planning – Creating a Safe Legal Haven for Families with Special Needs – SpecialPeopleSpecialPlanning.com

A Matter of Trust – The Importance of Personal Instructions – AmatterofTrust.info

Loving Without a License – An Estate Planning Survival Guide for Same Sex Couples and Unmarried Partners – LovingWithoutALicense.com

Women in Transition – Navigating the Legal and Financial Challenges in Your Life – WomenInTransitionToday.com

Like a Library Burning – Saving and Sharing Stories of a Lifetime – LikeALibraryBurning.com

Straight Talk! About Estate Planning – GratitudePartners.com

Straight Talk! What to Do When Someone Dies – GratitudePartners.com

What's The Deal With…Estate Planning – People Tested Media – PeopleTested.com

Whether to Wed, by Scott Squillace – WhetherToWed.com

Government Websites:

SSA.gov

IRS.gov

ABOUT THE AUTHOR

Peggy R. Hoyt, J.D., M.B.A, B.C.S.*

Florida board certified specialist in Wills, Trusts and Estates and Elder Law

Peggy is an attorney, author and entrepreneur who reflects her passion for pets in almost everything she does. She comes by her love of animals naturally as her father was the President and CEO of The Humane Society of the United States from 1970-1997.

Peggy and her law partner, Randy Bryan, own and operate The Law Offices of Hoyt & Bryan, LLC—Family Wealth & Legacy Counsellors, in Oviedo, Florida. Both Peggy and Randy are dual Florida Bar board certified specialists in Wills, Trusts and Estates as well as Elder Law. Their firm limits its practice to estate planning and elder law issues including the creation, maintenance and administration of estate plans that "work." Areas of expertise also include planning for special needs family members, unmarried couples, business succession and of course, pets.

Peggy has written a number of books. Her first, *All My Children Wear Fur Coats – How to Leave a Legacy for Your Pet*, (LegacyForYourPet.com) was inspired by her pets, currently three horses, seven dogs (including one retired service dog) and two cats. Other co-authored books include *Special*

People, Special Planning – Creating a Safe Legal Haven for Families with Special Needs; *Loving Without a License – An Estate Planning Survival Guide for Unmarried Couples and Same Sex Partners*; *A Matter of Trust – The Importance of Personal Instructions*; *Women in Transition – Navigating the Legal and Financial Challenges in Your Life*; *Like a Library Burning – Saving and Sharing Stories of a Lifetime*; *Thank Everybody for Everything – Grow Your Life and Business with Gratitude*; *Gratitude Expressions – a Five Year Journal*; and The Straight Talk Series that includes *Straight Talk! About Estate Planning* and *Straight Talk! What to Do When Someone Dies*. Her most recent book is *What's the Deal With… Estate Planning*. All are available on Amazon.com.

Peggy is active in a variety of organizations, including WealthCounsel, ElderCounsel, the Academy of Florida Elder Law Attorneys (AFELA), Central Florida Estate Planning Council and as an Executive Council member of the General Practice, Solo and Small Firm Section of the Florida Bar. She recently became a member of the Pet Loss Professionals Association, a division of the International Cemetery, Cremation and Funeral Association (ICCFA). She is a frequent speaker on estate planning and elder law topics, as well as practice management including team training and marketing.

Peggy is married to Joe Allen and spends her "free" time training for limited distance endurance and competitive trail riding events on her rescue Anglo Arab mare, Heaven.

To learn more or to contact Peggy:
Peggy@HoytBryan.com
HoytBryan.com
PeggyHoyt.com
@PeggyRHoyt
@PetLawyers